I'LL TELL YOU
ONE THING

by

**DAN
JENKINS**

Woodford Press

ISBN: 0-942627-56-3

Library of Congress Catalog Card Number: 99-65573

First printing, October, 1999
Printed and bound in the United States.
Distributed to the trade by Andrews McMeel Universal, Kansas City, MO.

Book Design by Jim Santore, Woodford Press.
Illustrations by Michel Bobot.

Woodford Press
5900 Hollis Street, Suite K
Emeryville, CA 94608
www.woodfordpub.com

Daniel C. Ross, CEO and Publisher
C. David Burgin, Editor and Publisher
William F. Duane, Senior Vice President

Associate Publishers:
Franklin M. Dumm
William W. Scott, Esq.
William B. McGuire, Esq.

ALSO BY DAN JENKINS

Novels
Rude Behavior
You Gotta Play Hurt
Fast Copy
Life Its Ownself
Baja Oklahoma
Limo (with Bud Shrake)
Dead Solid Perfect
Semi-Tough

Nonfiction
Fairways and Greens
Bubba Talks
You Call It Sports But I Say It's a Jungle Out There
Football (with Walter Iooss Jr.)
Saturday's America
The Dogged Victims of Inexorable Fate
The Best 18 Golf Holes in America
Greatest Moments in TCU Football History (with Francis J. Fitzgerald)
Sam Baugh: Best There Ever Was (with Whit Canning)
Doak Walker: More Than a Hero (with Whit Canning)
John David Crow: Heart of a Champion (with Steve Pate)
Darrell Royal: Dance With Who Brung You (with Mike Jones)

Screenplays
Baja Oklahoma (with Bobby Roth)
Dead Solid Perfect (with Bobby Roth)

Songs
Baja Oklahoma (with Willie Nelson)

Watching college football is the most
fun I ever had as a youngster. Covering
college football is the most fun I ever
had as a fully employed grownup.
I'LL TELL YOU ONE THING
is therefore dedicated to all those who've played the
college game, coached it, covered it, and
cared about it.

CONTENTS

This book is part fiction but mostly fact. The players in here are all real people, many of them larger than life. The great games they played did happen, and the incidents and things they said did occur. Everything in here, from scores to stats to quotes, is as accurate as a geezer could make it with the aid of his shelves of reference books, videotapes, eyeglasses, and magnifying glass. As for the fictitious characters who sneaked in here, all I can do is apologize for them. They just keep following me around.

— THE AUTHOR

FOREWORD

By Sally Jenkins

I t is not true that my father has turned into everything he used to make fun of. Just because he has endowed a scholarship at his alma mater, Texas Christian University, and he bought a new house specifically so he could see the TCU stadium from his living room, and he has his own monogrammed parking space there, and his walls are covered with vintage photographs of Davey O'Brien, and he treats the fortunes of the Horned Frogs as his own personal battle between good and evil, and he pores over old albums and annuals as if they were Plutarch, that doesn't make the man a fanatic, does it?

I hesitate to inform the reader that, a few years ago, a recruiting scandal struck TCU when it was discovered that some wealthy and influential alumni had a secret slush fund and were paying players in violation of NCAA rules. I was a young reporter with the *Washington Post*, assigned to cover college football. Determined to follow the story wherever it led me, I picked up the telephone and called home.

"Daddy," I said, "was it you?"

It wasn't. "But it could have been," he said.

When I went home to Fort Worth to visit my parents in their new house, I took in the grand view from their back porch, which consisted of the concrete upper tiers of TCU's stadium.

"Gee," I said, shading my eyes against the blazing sodium arena lights, "you can walk to games."

"No, I can't," my father said, scandalized. "What would I do with my parking space?"

There is just one thing Dan Jenkins loves as much as college football, and that is writing about it. Growing up, I thought all fathers were gone on the weekends and home on Tuesdays. I thought all fathers traveled to places like South Bend, University Park, College Station, Columbus, Norman and Lincoln, and liked it.

I thought all fathers ignored Thanksgiving, and toasted the New Year with a press-box hot dog at a bowl game. In our family, these holidays did not exist. Any resentment or psychological scarring I may have suffered was tempered by the fact that I was perfectly well aware — as an already discerning reader — that my father was in the process of writing hundreds of pieces considered classics of the genre, and becoming unanimously viewed as the most influential sportswriter of his generation, who would spawn scores of little imitators, not the least of whom would be, well, me.

Granted, I also thought all fathers wore Guccis with no socks, smoked five packs of cigarettes and drank 10 cups of coffee a day, and knew Joe Namath and Burt Reynolds, and wrote best-sellers on their summer vacations while snickering to themselves, and got invited to ride on Air Force One because the president loved his work.

But mainly, I thought all fathers must be the drop-dead funniest guys on earth. His idea of fatherly advice was, "Don't rob old people."

Once, he decided to caution my brother against a girl he was dating. "She looks like a speed trap to me," he said.

My father turned just reading the paper into an exercise in one-liners. Each morning he would sigh, rattling the pages, and say something like, "Big events in small minds."

Or, "The only time Margaret Thatcher cries is when she tries to comb her hair."

There are a lot of conventional things my father is no good at. Changing light bulbs, for instance, is a three-act comedy that usually ends with his three children in paroxysms of giggles. Putting up the Christmas tree, and getting it into its stand, was a yearly event that included both wails of laughter and a vale of tears. I remember vividly a charming Connecticut holiday when my mother had to clap her hands over my ears to protect me from the sound of my father struggling with and cursing an evergreen, which he was in the process of hacking into the size of a potted orchid. Inanimate objects tend to defy him with an obstinacy that seems almost personal, as if they know exactly who they are dealing with.

Suffice it to say, he was not a conventional father figure. He was not a lawn-mowing, hedge-trimming kind of Dad. He was not handy around the house, or good with the checkbook. He was more of an unindicted coconspirator. He was good at games. Battleship. Hot Wheels. Betting pools.

You name it.

And he has always been good at words. In my father's hands, words take on a life of their own. They fly out of typewriters and dance like the mops and brooms in the Disney cartoon *The Sorcerer's Apprentice.* He can make the little suckers do whatever he wants. They start and stop on a dime for him. Unless, of course, a key sticks, in which case I have seen him toss the entire typewriter into the garbage can.

For years, my father has defined autumn Saturdays and Sundays for millions of readers. In the golden age of *Sports Illustrated,* in the 1960s and 1970s, he brought national rivalries to a magazine that had previously only heard of the Harvard-Yale game. He at once popularized and chronicled the sport.

Some of my personal favorites:

After a Notre Dame loss, "Maybe the Vatican ought to consider banning Purdue instead of The Pill . . . And maybe Notre Dame would be better off trying to win one for Ara Parseghian instead of the Gipper."

Of Joe Namath, "Stoop-shouldered and sinisterly handsome, he slouched against the wall of the saloon, a filter cigarette in his teeth, collar open, perfectly happy and self-assured, gazing through the uneven darkness to sort out the winners from the losers . . . Sitting there, he seemed to pose a single question for all of us: Would you rather be young, single, rich, famous, talented, energetic and happy — or president?"

On the polls: "Back in the days when college football players wore those one-piece leather uniforms and ran with the dazzling speed of tree trunks, it was fairly easy to recognize the nation's No. 1 team every season."

What my father has to offer on the subject of football, above all, is authority. He combines a near-photographic memory with an eerie capacity to recite history on the page as if it comes from his own personal recollection. He once told me, "I have a nostalgia for times I didn't live in." The result is a writer with a hell of a one-two punch — he can recount the Princeton-Rutgers game as if he watched it from a buckboard wagon, and he really did see the first football game ever played on artificial turf in Knoxville, Tennessee.

He can tell you, off the top of his head, the winner of every Heisman Trophy. He can also tell you the winners of every major golf championship from its inception — and the runner-up. (It doesn't hurt, of course, that he has seen some two-score consecutive Masters firsthand.) To call his knowledge encyclopedic would be to trivialize it, because it is not just a mundane, catalog sort of knowledge. It always has a point, and context. For instance, he doesn't just recite Heisman Trophy winners — he tells you who should have won.

I am, of course, an extravagant admirer of his work.

But I am not alone. As has been noted by more than one critic, my father has an extremely disturbing habit of writing satire which then comes true. In his best-selling novel *Semi-Tough*, he dreamed up the most outlandishly excessive, smoke-and-pigeon filled Super Bowl halftime ceremony he could possibly think of, only to see it enacted in real life a couple of years later.

Whatever you are about to read, you can be certain that it either really did happen that way — or it is about to.

I will leave you with a phrase I heard my father utter often when I was growing up.

"I could be wrong," he would say. "But I'm not."

Sally Jenkins has written for Women's Sports and Fitness, GQ *and* ESPN *magazines. An alumnus of Stanford, she has worked for* The Washington Post *and* Sports Illustrated.

ONE

T.J. LAMBERT said if he wanted a sense of history he'd have paid more attention in class to goofy old Dr. Bundhanke when the professor talked about your light-running ethnics.

"Mohammed and them," T.J. said. "Your stove lids, bedsheets. All them people who kept getting conquered by Attila the Hun or King Tut. Some dwarf in sandals who slept with a dagger in his teeth. Conquered people, made everybody eat raw pigeon, talk in hieroglyphics."

Tommy Earl Bruner said, "I generally do my best to steer clear of a dwarf who sleeps with a dagger in his teeth. He'll try to conquer your ass ever chance he gets."

"Bird, rock, doodad," T.J. said. "What it looks like, your hieroglyphics. Man comes in your office, carves a rock, a stick, and a doodad on your wall, you're supposed to know what he means?"

"You could just nod," Tommy Earl said.

"What if I want to talk back?" T.J. asked.

"Tell him roof, rope, dog, curly thing," said Tommy Earl. "Just say it, you don't have to carve it. Then the two of you can lapse into an interesting conversation about pyramids ... Hindus ... Babylon ... Cleopatra ... who she's jacking around with these days."

T.J. said to Tommy Earl, "So I just go up and say, 'Hey, there, Abdul, old buddy. Roof, rope, doodad, stick — and I wonder if you happen to know the score of the TCU-Southern Cal game?' That it?"

Tommy Earl shook his head, fondled a Winston. "Scores ain't in yet. What with looking out for dinosaurs, it takes a year to chisel scores in the wall of the cave. First your hieroglyphic man has to figure out what a Frog and a Trojan look like. That's so he can chisel 'em up there with his bird, rock, and doodad."

Billy Clyde Puckett spoke up, saying he'd often wondered where the hieroglyphic man went to buy the tools to chisel with. Tut's Ace Hardware, maybe, over on the south side of Cairo.

He went on, "I imagine it was fairly inconvenient to live in a time before newspapers you could get the scores in, or even before the sausage and egg biscuit at Hardees, for that matter."

T.J. said, "Might as well be a chink as a hieroglyphic man. Talk in dots and slashes."

"Well, except for the fact that all your chinks don't talk in dots and dashes," Tommy Earl said. "Your Jap chink talks in pieces of broken lumber. Your Chinese chink talks in bean sprouts and crinkly wontons. I guess there's some chinks over there somewhere who talk in dots and dashes. I'm just not all that up on it."

We were in He's Not Here, a convivial spot in Fort Worth.

It was one of those joints where Patsy Cline was still alive and lived inside the jukebox, where the barmaid was a rack-loaded wool-driver, where they enforced this intelligent rule that said if you wanted to not smoke, you had to go outdoors.

Over by the filling-station clock and the poster of Humphrey Bogart and Ingrid Bergman was where you could still find my 10 Stages of Drunkenness, after all these years. Inside a nice frame you could read:

The 10 Stages of Drunkenness

1. Witty and Charming.
2. Rich and Powerful.
3. Benevolent.
4. Clairvoyant.
5. Fuck Dinner.
6. Patriotic.
7. Crank Up the Enola Gay.
8. Witty and Charming, Part II.
9. Invisible.
10. Bulletproof.

The rack-loaded wool-driver behind the bar was Tami Kay Mitchell. She'd been a TCU cheerleader in the Seventies, back when there wasn't much TCU football to cheer about. That was also before cheerleaders had to do Mary Lou Rettons. Just look good. She'd married a TCU linebacker who thought he'd make it in the NFL, but didn't. He became a weed-growing biker instead. Tami Kay spent some time riding on the back of his Harley, going to biker rallies down on the Gulf Coast.

It took her a while to discover her husband was "about half-crude and semi-useless." She finally dropped a Tammy Wynette on him — and said the last straw was a T-shirt he wore one day on his bike.

The message on the back of it said:

IF YOU CAN READ THIS, THE BITCH FELL OFF

This was the day before the big TCU-USC game. The Frogs, winners of Conference USA, had been chosen by the computer as one of the eight teams

Texas A&M's John Kimbrough

The Longhorns' Jack Crain

SMU's Doak Walker

going into the NCAA's national championship playoff, and they drew Southern Cal in the first round.

TCU Stadium had been chosen as the site for reasons that had to do with the TV network's time zones and other games.

The other six teams in the playoffs were Ohio State, Tennessee, Florida State, Miami, Texas, and Notre Dame. The computer didn't pick Notre Dame, which had a 4-7 record. The playoff committee did. The committee comprised baby boomers and yuppies and their tune-deaf offspring at the TV network. Better for ratings if the Fighting Irish were in the playoffs, they contended.

Notre Dame, of course, is the only school that's never played a game away from home. They always have you outnumbered with their subway Catholics and nuns. That's why you often hear people say, "My two favorite teams are my alma mater and whoever's playing Notre Dame Saturday."

If you'd ever read the letters to the editor in newspapers and magazines or got yourself on the electric computer net, you'd know that America's boomers and yuppies think a playoff is better than letting polls decide the football champion of the USA, even if it means Notre Dame will be in the playoffs every season.

But if you ask a geezer or codger about it, somebody like me, a man who'd been vigorously keeping up with college football since leather helmets, you'll hear that most boomers and yuppies didn't know diddly about anything but the Nasdaq and fish tacos.

My educated guess was, no boomer or yuppie had ever named a son Doak or Slingin' Sam.

On those rare occasions when I'd run into a boomer who'd actually be familiar with the exploits of such immortals as SMU's Doak Walker, "the Mustang Miracle Man," TCU's Slingin' Sam Baugh, "the Sweetwater Six-Shooter," and Davey (Slingshot) O'Brien, "the Dallas Dynamo," or Texas A&M's Jarrin' John Kimbrough, "the Haskell Hurricane," or the University of Texas' Jackrabbit Jack Crain, "the Nocona Nugget," I'd sink to my knees and thank the Skipper for delaying the end of civilization a while longer. There was still hope for the world. Youth didn't entirely consist of computer zombies and noise-music robots.

I'm a poll man. Born a poll man. Raised a poll man. I remember a time when there was only AP, no UP. I even remember a time when there wasn't even an AP poll, just the two syndicated authorities, the Dickinson Rating

System and the Williamson Rankings. They rated the nation's teams with an arithmetic formula on a weekly basis during the season and eventually let their arithmetic decide the national champion.

What did it matter some seasons if the polls disagreed, if more than one team was named No. 1? All you had to lose was more bumper stickers.

Billy Clyde, T.J., and Tommy Earl were hearing this again at the bar in He's Not Here. They were obligated to listen, seeing as how I'd done wonders for their careers.

Some people in Fort Worth insisted that Billy Clyde, T.J., and Tommy Earl wouldn't even exist if it hadn't been for me.

That wasn't necessarily a compliment. It depended on whether you liked to read books that I said were romantic comedies and other people said were dirty. Whether you liked books about sporting fellows and shapely adorables or dull novels about dreary people written by psychobabble men with beards and rodent-women in sack dresses and granny glasses.

It also might depend on whether you preferred barbecue at the Railhead and enchiladas at Mi Cocinita over mushroom pilaf with decaf calamari and zucchini flan.

I said to the group, "I'll tell you one thing. If you think this TCU-Southern Cal game is big ..."

But Tommy Earl cut me off, saying, "He's gonna tell us about the Thirties. I'm sure of it."

TCU's Sam Baugh

TCU's Davey O'Brien, the 1938 Heisman winner.

TWO

I T'S TRUE, I was. Even so, their faces didn't glaze over. Long as they could get an Abbot-rocks, Curtis-soda, or Junior-water, fire up a smoke, and have a rack-loaded wool-driver to look at, they couldn't be bored.

The Thirties were the longest decade. They started with the Wall Street crash of '29 and didn't end till Pearl Harbor in '41. Bust me.

The Thirties were also my favorite decade. Not because I was partial to dust bowls or certain people having to eat grapes on wrath or on Mrs. Baird's light bread, it was because so many things were better in the Thirties.

Cars were better. They didn't all look like a Lexus. You had your white Cords, your yellow LaSalles, your burgundy Packards, your top-down Duesenburgs, and the best car I ever owned, the green '36 Ford Roadster. Convertible, rumble seat, big white sidewalls, stick shift, running boards, spare on the back.

Gangsters were better. Who wouldn't take a Baby Face Nelson, Pretty Boy Floyd, Bonnie and Clyde, Ma Barker, John Dillinger, Paul Muni, James Cagney, or Edward G. Robinson over a Michael Milken?

Movies were better. Who wouldn't rather watch Bette Davis smoke two cigarettes at once before she went blind or shot somebody instead of car chases, mutant wars, or rich teenagers giving each other cute-mouth?

In the Thirties you could get frosted mugs of root beer from carhops on roller skates who looked like Priscilla Lane. The big department stores then were as exotic as Disney World today. Night clubs were where orchestras played songs with melodies, and Cafe Society dressed up like Cary Grant and Jean Harlow and went to the nightclubs to drink champagne and idly smoke cigarettes instead of voting for your liberals and adopting Albanians.

No neighborhood, street, highway, building, or city was ever crowded, and bridal paths frequently ran down the center of tree-lined thoroughfares.

You could travel almost anywhere on a sleek passenger train, a 20th Century Limited, Burlington Zephyr, or Sunshine Special, and play bridge in your private compartment with Carole Lombard, Norma Shearer, and Paulette Goddard, or have a highball in the club car with Clark Gable, and not have to worry about a towelhead planting a bomb on board.

Newspapers were better because there were hundreds more of them around. Every city had at least three, and some cities had 14 or more. The papers had lots of space for all the news and they printed big pictures of football players stiff-arming the world and beautiful young ladies sitting on horses, and people like Grantland Rice and Damon Runyon wrote for them.

And then there was radio. Day and night, everybody listened to the radio for entertainment, or maybe just to get the grain reports. America listened to "One Man's Family," "Big Town," "I Love a Mystery," Jack Benny, Fred Allen, "Vic and Sade," "Amos 'n' Andy," "Easy Aces," not to forget "Our Gal Sunday," "Young Widder Brown," "Lorenzo Jones," and "Stella Dallas," and not to overlook the powerhouse afternoon lineup of "Buck Rogers," "Dick Tracy," "Jack Armstrong," "Little Orphan Annie," and "The Lone Ranger."

Radio then was better than TV today. Radio made you use your imagination. TV makes you use your clicker.

Listening to "One Man's Family" on the radio every Sunday evening, sponsored by Tenderleaf Tea, written by Carlton E. Morse, I was sure I knew exactly what they all looked like when Father Barber was in the study saying, "Yes, yes, Fanny," and Paul was in the library trying to figure out how to break it off with Beth Holly, and Hazel was in the kitchen, and

TCU's All-America quarterback Sam Baugh.

Claudia was out in the garden with Nicholas Lacy, and Clifford was daydreaming down on the seawall, and Hank and Pinky were up at the Sky Ranch.

"Do 'The Shadow,'" Tommy Earl said.

"'The Shadow'?" I said. "Lamont Cranston? A man of wealth, a student of science, a master of other peoples' minds? The Shadow has devoted his life to righting wrongs, protecting the innocent, punishing the guilty. He uses advanced methods that might ultimately become available to all law enforcement agencies. He's never seen, only heard, as haunting to superstitious minds as a ghost, as inevitable as a guilty conscience. He's ably assisted in conquering evil by his friend and constant companion, the lovely Margo Lane. In tonight's episode ..."

T.J. said, "I like that Mr. District Attorney deal."

I responded, "And it shall be my duty as District Attorney not only to prosecute all persons accused of crimes perpetrated within this county but to defend with equal vigor the rights and privileges of all its citizens ... with Vicki Vola as Miss Miller and Len Doyle as Harrington."

Billy Clyde said, "Grand Central Station's my favorite."

I quickly said, "As a bullet seeks its target, shining rails in every part of our great country are aimed at Grand Central Station, heart of the nation's greatest city. Drawn by the magnetic force of the fantastic metropolis, day and night great trains rush toward the Hudson River, sweep down its eastern bank for a hundred and forty miles, flash briefly by the long red row of tenement houses south of 125th Street, dive with a roar into the two-and-a-half-mile tunnel which burrows beneath the glitter and swank of Park Avenue, and then ... Grand Central Station. Crossroads of a million private lives — a gigantic stage on which are played a thousand dramas daily."

Football announcers were certainly better in the Thirties. They not only could invent emergency laterals when they had to — when they'd realize they had the wrong guy headed for a touchdown — they could make a 20-yard run sound like it went 50 yards, and a 50-yard run sound like the tornado that wiped out half of Oklahoma City.

There was no better treat on a Saturday afternoon than hearing the industrious Kern Tips broadcasting the Humble Oil and Refining Company's Southwest Conference Game of the Week, if for no other reason than to hear him say, "He's a piston-legged package of dynamite, a rolling bundle of butcher knives — down at Aggieland they call him Dangerous Dick Todd, the Crowell Cyclone."

Almost everything was better in the Thirties, except, I suppose, if you want to be particular, air-conditioning.

There were times in the Thirties where the only place you could go to cool off in the summer would be the Parkway Theater when you went to see a serial with the Green Hornet and his trusty sidekick, Kato.

T.J. said, "Wasn't Kato some kind of chink?"

THREE

EVERYTHING WE know today tells us that if you can get a kid interested in sports at an early age, the odds are in your favor that he won't wind up with a ring in his nose or his tongue pierced.

It doesn't always work but I know a gang of football immortals had a positive influence on me as a kid. I don't think I'd ever have wound up with a ring in my nose or a piece of costume jewelry stuck in my tongue under any circumstances, barring whiskey, but seeing those heroes live and in action had something to do with making me want to try to achieve something big or little in the world of sports someday instead of trying to be Al Capone, or, perhaps even worse, a politician.

Surely I'm one of the few people still on the planet who actually saw with my own eyes, right there in TCU stadium, high up on the north end of the west stands, the 1935 TCU-SMU game. That game still gets voted onto the list when lofty panels go about naming the 10 greatest college games ever played.

Even at the age of 7, thanks to the reporting of dads, uncles, and older cousins, I

TCU's Jimmy Lawrence roars around the end against the Mustangs in 1935's "Game of the Century."

TCU's Tillie Manton knifes through the SMU line.

Horned Frogs reserve Scott McCall eludes a pony.

knew that the game on November 30, 1935, was between two undefeated, untied teams, that it was for the national championship as well as the Southwest Conference championship, that the winner would be invited to the Rose Bowl, and that two great, gallant, sensational, and otherwise stupendous All-American backs would be on the field, they being TCU's Slingin' Sam Baugh and SMU's Will 'o' the Wisp Bobby Wilson, "the Corsicana Comet."

The memory now coexists with facts later learned.

TCU stadium held only 30,000 in those days, there was no upper deck on the west side, and the end zones were grassy slopes. The game had been a sellout for weeks, but to accommodate the hysterical demand for tickets, temporary bleachers holding 2,500 each were erected in the end zones.

Still, on the day of the game, excited mobs assaulted the grounds. Fans drove their cars through the wire fence that surrounded the stadium, and other fans leaped over the fence from the tops of automobiles, scattering in all directions and pushing into the stadium to create standing room for themselves.

Before that, scalpers had sold tickets for $100 each, and this was in the middle of the Great Depression when hamburgers were a nickel, movies were a dime, and a five-course dinner in an elegant restaurant was $1.25.

The crowd was estimated at somewhere between 37,000 and 42,000. In any case, on that day it was the largest crowd ever to see a football game in the state of Texas. The throng not only included a cluster of celebrities from stage and screen, but a choice group of famous coaches from around the nation.

Among the coaches who came to see what Southwest Conference football was

TCU Stadium on November 30, 1935, when nation's gridiron spotlight moved to Fort Worth.

all about were Minnesota's Bernie Bierman, Northwestern's Pappy Waldorf, Oklahoma's Biff Jones, California's Stub Allison, and Indiana's Bo McMillin, a Fort Worth native, by the way.

To handle the press, radio, and newsreel coverage a special makeshift open-air press box was built on top of the east stands, and one could only guess at how crowded the main press box was. Bill Stern his ownself was there to broadcast the game for Mutual radio. So were Kern Tips and his "color man," Cy Leland, TCU's first great running back of '29 and '30. They called the game for NBC. These were the first coast-to-coast broadcasts of a Southwest Conference game.

And no college sports information director would have wanted to be TCU's J. Willard

Rice's Bill Wallace, "the Eagle Lake Express," was the first Southwest back to make AP and *Collier's* All-America, in 1934.

Ridings that Saturday. It was Ridings who had to worry about seating for the nation's sportswriting elite. Almost every big-time byliner was in town, like it was a heavyweight championship fight.

This impressive lineup of sportswriters would quickly type up deadline yarns on the game and hand the copy over to Western Union or Postal Telegraph operators who in turn would, through the miracle of electricity, punch out the stories to newspapers across the land.

Grantland Rice of the *New York Sun* and the NANA syndicate was the most celebrated writer in the box, but some of the other "names" present were Paul Gallico of *The New York Journal-American*, Joe Williams of *The New York World-Telegram*, Allison Danzig of *The New York Times*, Bill Cunningham of *The*

Boston Globe, Harry Grayson of NEA, Prescott Sullivan of the *San Francisco Examiner*, Maxwell Stiles of *The Los Angeles Mirror*, Lloyd Gregory of *The Houston Post*, Alan Gould of the AP, and Henry McLemore of UP.

Only one other event in the entire history of the city had ever circulated the Fort Worth dateline so widely. That was back in 1918 during World War I when Vernon Castle, the internationally famous ballroom dancer, had been killed in a plane crash during a training flight at an air base for Royal Canadian fighter pilots on the southwest side of town.

The fact is, I'd been in the stadium only a week before to see a game that was almost as big, the one where TCU at 9-0 met the defending conference champion Rice Owls at 8-1. Earlier in the season, before a narrow loss to SMU, Rice had been No. 1 in the nation in the Williamson Rankings.

I'd been told to look out for Rice's "Touchdown Twins," halfback Bill Wallace, "the Eagle Lake Express," and quarterback John McCauley, "the Hubbard Havoc." Both had been All-Americans in '34. In fact, Bill Wallace in '34 became the first backfield ace from the Southwest Conference to make Granny Rice's All-America team in Collier's as well as the AP All-America, they being the two most respected selections.

But Wallace and McCauley weren't the league's first All-Americans, if I can interrupt myself.

It's generally agreed that the Southwest Conference "came of age," as they say, in the season of 1927 when TCU's notorious end Rags Matthews, Texas A&M's triple-threat halfback Joel Hunt, and SMU's gifted quarterback Gerald Mann, "the little red arrow," all were named to some lesser selections, but their big lick came when they were invited to the East-West Shrine game in San Francisco.

They dominated it, is what they did. They led the West all-stars to a 16-to-6 victory over a squad of Easterners that included Yale's All-America back, Bruce Caldwell. Hunt and Mann each scored a touchdown, but it was Matthews who made himself so all-around indiscreet that day he was named the game's MVP. Rags was so outstanding the headline in one of San Francisco's papers, the *Call-Bulletin*, said:

MATTHEWS BEATS EAST.

All-Americans came easier to the Southwest after that.

SMU Guard Choc Sanders and University of Texas Tackle Gordy Brown made notable teams in 1928.

TCU guard Mike Brumbelow, SMU tackle Marion (Scrapiron) Hammon, and Arkansas end Wear Schoonover were selected on prominent teams in 1929, a season which saw the Frogs, with the swift Cy Leland averaging 7.2 yards a carry, go unbeaten (9-0-1), win their first conference title, and find themselves listed among the nation's top five teams in a national AP roundup.

The season of 1930 saw the Baylor guard, Barton (Bochey) Koch, mayhem his way into Baylor legend. With a name that didn't hurt him at all, he became the conference's first consensus All-America. TCU's Leland made at least one team that year, the selector perhaps paying Leland back for having overlooked his more spectacular junior season.

Two of the Southwest's most renowned backs of the early Thirties were SMU's Weldon (Speedy) Mason and the University of Texas' Harrison Stafford. Mason made one All-America team in '31 and Stafford made one in '32, and their fans said justice had finally been served.

Also in '32, TCU's Johnny Vaught, a rugged guard on a championship team (10-0-1) that wound up No. 4 in the land, became the first conference player to make the AP All-America. This was the same Johnny Vaught who went on to coach all those great teams at Ole Miss in the Forties and Fifties.

Let's see, where'd I leave off? Oh, yeah.

Although it was unknown to me at the time, it was those same Rice Owls I was getting ready to watch in '35 who combined with some Texas Longhorns the year before to get the full attention of the press "up north."

On the Saturday of October 6, 1934, only 100 miles apart in the same state of Indiana, the Longhorns knocked off heavily favored Notre Dame 7 to 6 in South Bend while the Owls mistreated heavily favored Purdue 14 to 0 in West Lafayette.

This was colossal stuff. Football in the Lone Star state had never known such notoriety, especially from your undeniably biased Easterners, Northerners, Northeasterners, Midwesterners, and assorted Damn Yankees.

SMU's All-America Bobby Wilson darts through Frogs in the 1935 classic.

Against a Notre Dame team that was building up to being ferocious, fashioning an attack around Bill Shakespeare and Andy Pilney, the Longhorns countered with not much more than their broken-field stud, Bohn Hilliard, "the Orange Flash," who could only have come from Orange, Texas.

Hilliard was enough. His legs and his toe. He ran nine yards for the touchdown, then booted the extra-point for the winning margin.

Meanwhile, over in West Lafayette, Coach Noble Kizer's Purdue team had been the preseason pick for No. 1, primarily because their triple-threat All-America tailback had returned, a guy named Duane Purvis, and the Boilermakers had lost only four games in the past five seasons. But Rice's "Touchdown Twins" got together to break up a scoreless tie in the fourth quarter. They combined on a 57-yard touchdown pass, Wallace to McCauley, and that alone was enough to dust off the Boilermakers, who gave up another touchdown in the final moments on a fumble.

The Rice team of '34 was spoken of with solemn reverence for many years, and not just because of the "Touchdown Twins." Even hobos who came to your back door to get food and water could recite the Owls' lineup: ends Leche Sylvester and Bobby Forbes, tackles Primo Miller and Rayburn Mays, guards Red Bale and Carmen Brandon, center Percy Arthur, and backs Wallace, McCauley, Buck Friedman and Harry Witt.

The Owls finished with a 9-1-1 record that season, wound up ranked No. 4 in the country by Williamson, even received Rose Bowl "feelers," and were mainly responsible for inspiring the radio broadcasts of Southwest Conference games.

After the Owls and Longhorns had done those wonderful things to Notre Dame and Purdue, their collision with each other on October 27 at Rice Field in Houston — capacity only 18,000 then — caused such a ticket frenzy it created the first Southwest Conference Game of the Week on radio.

People listened to a dandy. Texas led 9 to 7 on a Bohn Hilliard field goal with only three minutes to play, but that's when Bill Wallace flipped a 76-yard touchdown pass, and in the final seconds Rice intercepted a Texas pass for another touchdown, making the final score 20 to 9.

But all that was throat-clearing.

This, you see, was virtually the same Rice team that I watched TCU whip up on in '35 by the score of 27 to 6, as the Frogs warmed up for SMU. Slingin' Sam Baugh and Jimmy Lawrence, a tough all-around back, destroyed the Owls even though Bill Wallace ran around this way and that in his satin pants for 140 yards.

I might mention that my dad was a diehard TCU fan. Bud Jenkins, as friends knew him, was a handsome dude of casual attire. He generally wore checkered sport coats, open-collar shirts, carried a dimpled silver pocket flask, and drove convertibles. He was a good furniture salesman, but my mother, the former Catherine Louise O'Hern, who was in charge of Lucky Strike cigarettes, black coffee, and antiques, felt he never let work interfere with a round of golf, a card game, or going to a sports event.

It's still easy to recall being astounded by the vastness of TCU's stadium, a veritable concrete giant with a beautiful lawn that looked better than anybody's front yard I'd ever romped on. It was hard to imagine how a bigger stadium could exist anywhere, not even if you went to the zoo and brought back all kinds of lions and Christians to put in it.

At the Rice game I think I was even more dazzled by the uniforms on the gladiators than I was by the stadium.

The Frogs wore white jerseys with purple numerals, light khaki pants with the wide purple stripe up the back, and shiny black helmets, but the Owls looked even slicker in their royal blue jerseys with white numerals, bright gold helmets with blue trim, and deep gold satin pants.

It was a mistake to mention to Bud Jenkins that the Owls' uniforms looked a lot fancier than TCU's. All it got from him was a look.

A Saturday later in the stadium that was now overflowing for the SMU-TCU game, the biggest game in the history of the state, I made the same mistake, saying I liked SMU's uniforms better than TCU's, even better than Rice's.

The Mustangs were wearing polished red helmets, two-tone pants that were red knit in back and sort of a canvas-khaki color in front, and their jerseys were red with blue numerals and had these wide blue stripes that ran up the ribcages from the waist to the armpits.

"Just eat your hot dog," my dad said. "You don't know what you're talking about."

Then this guy, Bud Jenkins, who'd once won a dance contest with Fort Worth's Ginger Rogers and played rounds of golf with Fort Worth's Ben Hogan, took another swig from his flask of what he called "cough medicine."

The game was such a classic and has become so much a part of gridiron lore, the lineups are hereby preserved in hardcover.

TCU		SMU
L.D. Meyer	LE	Bill Tipton
Drew Ellis	LT	Truman Spain
Cotton Harrison	LG	J.C. (Ironman) Wetsel
Darrell Lester	C	Art Johnson
Tracy Kellow.	RG	Billy Stamps
Wilson Groseclose	RT	Maurice Orr
Walter Roach	RE	Maco Stewart
Sam Baugh	Q	Johnny Sprague
Dutch Kline	LH	Bobby Wilson
Jimmy Lawrence	RH	Shelley Burt
Tillie Manton	F	Bob Finley

Five of those guys had already been selected All-Americans before the big day arrived. For the Frogs, they were Baugh and center Darrell Lester, who had just become the first two-year consensus All-America in conference history. For the Mustangs, they were the speedy little do-it-all halfback Bobby Wilson, tackle Truman Spain, and Guard J.C. (Ironman) Wetsel.

Their season records at kickoff time were awesome.

TCU		(10-0)	SMU		(10-0)
41	Howard Payne	0	39	North Texas State	0
28	North Texas State	11	60	Austin College	0
13	Arkansas	7	14	Tulsa	0
13	Tulsa	0	35	Washington U. (Mo.)	6
19	Texas A&M	14	10	Rice	0
27	Centenary	7	18	Hardin-Simmons	6
28	Baylor	0	20	Texas	0
14	Loyola (La.)	0	21	UCLA	0
28	Texas	0	17	Arkansas	6
27	Rice	6	10	Baylor	0

Helping to fire up the alumni and fans of the two schools was the geographic fact that Fort Worth and Dallas were only 30 miles apart, and were rival cities to begin with.

Dallas had already been chosen as the official site for the upcoming Texas Centennial celebration of 1936 — an enormous deal — and this had annoyed the hell out of Fort Worth's bidness leaders.

Specifically, it annoyed the hell out of Amon Carter Sr., the wealthy Fort Worth owner and publisher of the *Star-Telegram*, a man deservedly known as the "father of Fort Worth." It annoyed him so much he thought up the Fort Worth Frontier Centennial that would open at the same time and compete with the Dallas pageant. To do this Carter hired the prestigious Broadway showman Billy Rose to arrange the entertainment.

SMU's Matty Bell chats with TCU's Dutch Meyer before the Big One in 1935.

This would ultimately result in Billy Rose creating Casa Mañana, a mammoth outdoor dinner theater, Pioneer Palace, a rowdy dance hall and vaudeville show, Jumbo, the Broadway musical, and The Last Frontier, an outdoor rodeo-pageant where cowboys killed Indians every night.

Billy Rose hired all kinds of show biz stars. Paul Whiteman and his orchestra along with "100 of Texas' Most Beautiful Girls" were the feature attractions at the astounding Casa Mañana, which seated 4,500 customers who dined and drank and enjoyed lavish production numbers on a big stage that revolved on a pool of water.

Other artists who came to town were Everett Marshall, the Broadway tenor, Frances Langford, the pop singer, Ann Pennington, the Broadway musical star, Eddie Foy Jr., the dancer-comedian, and Sally Rand, the fan dancer who was unquestionably the main attraction at Sally Rand's Nude Ranch, another Billy Rose creation.

Dallas got even more irritated when Billy Rose came up with the advertising slogan, "Dallas for Culture, Fort Worth for Fun."

This seemed to make sense, especially after Sally Rand arrived in Fort Worth and said to the press and greeting committee, "I'm just a tan, blonde, big-bosomed, bubble-butted, sexy female. Hiya, Texas!"

But back to the Poll Bowl of '35.

To top everything off, the two syndicated rating systems came out the week of the game. They revealed that TCU was No. 1 in the nation in Williamson, and SMU was No. 1 in Dickinson.

I wouldn't presume to be able to tell the story of the game better than the most famous sportswriter on hand, so for a few moments I'll turn it over to His Grantlandness:

By GRANTLAND RICE

(Copyright 1935, by NANA, Inc.)

FORT WORTH, Texas, Nov. 30 — In the most desperate football this season has known from coast to coast, Southern Methodist beat Texas Christian 20 to 14 today, and thereby carved out a clear-cut highway to the Rose Bowl beyond any argument or doubt.

In the Fort Worth stadium that seated 30,000 spectators over 40,000 wildly excited Texans and visitors from every corner of the map packed, jammed and fought their way into every square foot of standing and seating space to see one of the greatest football games ever played in the 60-year history of the Nation's finest college sport.

Terrific line play by fast young giants, hard-driving and elusive running backs, forward passing that electrified the packed stands — especially by TCU's

Sammy Baugh — hard blocking and tackling, and magnificent kicking turned this climax game of 1935 into a combination of all-around skill and drama no other football crowd has seen.

With the Rose Bowl at stake, Southern Methodist got the big jump by taking a lead of 14 to 0. In the first period Bob Finley, filling in for the injured Harry Shuford, dashed over the line at the end of a 73-yard march featuring a tricky arsenal of reverses, plunges, and laterals.

In the second period SMU scored again on a 33-yard pass from Finley to Maco Stewart and Bobby Wilson's 9-yard sprint around end.

Facing this smothering margin Texas Christian came back from the middle of the second period with a counter charge that almost swept the Mustangs off the field.

This attack was led by the brilliant passing of Sam Baugh, who fired the leather with as much speed as Dizzy Dean ever knew, and the driving runs of Jimmy Lawrence. Two long TCU drives stalled but on a third one Lawrence finally fought his way across from the 4-yard line for the first touchdown. Trailing 14 to 7 at the top of the fourth period, Lawrence again climaxed a long drive with the tying score as Baugh whipped the ball into his arms from just outside the 5-yard line.

Tied at 14 to 14, the crowd sensed a TCU victory against a fading SMU team, but Jimmy Lawrence was lost to the Horned Frogs with an ankle injury on his second touchdown, which offset the absence of Shuford in the SMU line-up. In any case, it was the Mustangs who had the winning drive left.

With seven minutes to play, and facing a fourth down and 7 yards to go at the TCU 37-yard line, Southern Methodist pulled the most daring play of a daring game. In place of punting, Finley suddenly fell back and pegged a 50-yard aerial down the field.

Bobby Wilson, the greatest running back of 1935, raced for the goal-line with TCU's Harold McClure, subbing for Lawrence, in close pursuit. As the ball came over Wilson's shoulder, the 150-pound back made a leaping, diving catch that swept him across the line for the winning score. It was a great pass but an even greater catch.

SMU missed the extra-point in the excitement, which gave TCU hope in the fading minutes. Sam Baugh's passing attack twice carried the Frogs into SMU territory in the last few moments but they couldn't score. In fact, Baugh's passes were eating up ground at the Mustangs' 25-yard line when the final whistle blew, and SMU supporters were almost in a panic from this deathly machine-gun fire.

The terrific attack in this game is shown by the count of 25 first downs for TCU and 17 for SMU. The two teams gained almost 700 yards from scrimmage between them. They were the two most spectacular, all-around teams I have seen this year.

Your basic postscripts:

★ Of all the great moments that occurred in the 80-year history of the Southwest Conference, the Bobby Wilson "catch" for the winning touchdown is still considered the greatest play of all.

Years afterward, Bobby wrote me a letter that said in part: "There's one small detail about the game that people never knew. The man who deserves credit for calling that winning pass was J.R. (Jackrabbit) Smith. He suggested it in the huddle and no one contested.

"The only thing I did was remind Bob Finley to be sure to throw the ball far enough that it would go over the goal in case I missed it. In those days a pass over the goal was the same as a kick. The ball came out to the 20.

"I ran straight out to the right, then cut fast down the sideline, and I believe that if I had missed the pass it would have gone over the goal."

It was also years afterward that Kern Tips, the broadcaster, tried to correct some of the myths that had grown up around the "catch." In a book of his own, *Football Texas Style*, he wrote:

"While the ball was in the air, some will tell you that Wilson stopped, turned and came back for it; some that he kept running; some that he looked over his shoulder from the 10, to the 6, to the 4-yard line, trying to find the ball. So I shall put in my two cents worth. Wilson never swerved from the straight sideline path, and on the TCU 3-yard line he looked back, leaped high in the air, tipped down the football into control, and hugged onto it as he scrambled into the TCU end zone, glad to be alive and part of a miracle."

★ TCU's Dutch Meyer, who was only in his second year as a head coach, took the blame for the loss. He admitted he got outcoached by SMU's Matty Bell, a Fort Worth native, who was far more experienced. Matty had been the head coach for six years at TCU and five years at Texas A&M before he took over from Ray Morrison at SMU. Dutch had made a fiery, sermon-type pregame talk to the Frogs and sent them out on the field wound up so tight they had tears in their eyes. In the game's early stages, this resulted in the Frogs playing tentative defense — their feet might as well have been in cement — and on offense they clearly dropped over a dozen of Sam Baugh's passes. For the day, they caught only 19 of 44.

In contrast, Matty Bell had sent the Mustangs out loose and laughing. As he said later, "I didn't have to tell 'em it was a big game — they knew it."

★ Already crowned the nation's No. 1 team at the end of the regular season by the Dickinson System, and ceremonially presented with the Knute Rockne Trophy that went with it — giving the Southwest Conference its first national championship team in history — SMU seemed to take the Rose Bowl game against Stanford far too casually, as more of a Hollywood excursion than a football game. The Mustangs were heavily favored, after all, having gone out to Los Angeles earlier in the season and defeated a UCLA team 21 to 0 that had beaten Stanford 7 to 6.

On top of that, many SMU players had loaded up on Rose Bowl tickets they hoped to sell for minor fortunes. Bad idea. An unfortunate traffic jam involving many of the 85,000 fans kept the Mustangs from arriving at the Rose Bowl until 20 minutes before the kickoff. They barely had time to suit up while they ate the game tickets.

As a consequence, the Ponies put on a dreary exhibition. They stopped their own drives with seven turnovers, one of them a fumble at the Stanford 3-yard line on first down, and embarrassingly lost the whole game 7 to 0.

★ That upset was a good deal for the Frogs. As a consolation prize, they'd gone to the Sugar Bowl in New Orleans, which was where they defeated a powerful LSU team that was rated No. 3 in the nation. The Frogs won in the drizzle and mud by the baseball score of 3 to 2. Tillie Manton's field goal with Sam Baugh holding was the difference. But it hadn't been that close, really. Kicking with a wet ball, Sam averaged 45 yards on 14 punts that day, constantly keeping the Tigers deep in their own territory, and after reeling off a curving 44-yard run, the longest of the game by far, Baugh had driven the Frogs down to the lip of the LSU goal where they were poised to score again as the game ended.

In the end, TCU and SMU both finished with 12-1 records, and the combination of SMU losing to Stanford and TCU beating LSU boosted the Frogs up to No. 1 in the Williamson system's post-bowl tabulations.

This marked the first time — and one of only three times ever — that two Southwest Conference football teams in the same season could boast of a national championship.

And the publication of the Final Williamson Rankings in the *Fort Worth Star-Telegram* on January 12 gave old Bud Jenkins an occasion to drink some more of his "cough medicine," but for an altogether happier reason.

SMU'S 1935 NATIONAL CHAMPIONS

Halfback
J.R. (Jackrabbit)
Smith

Halfback
Shelley
Burt

All-America halfback
Bobby Wilson

All-America
guard
J.C. (Ironman)
Wetsel

Center
Art Johnson

End
Bill
Tipton

All-America
tackle
Truman
Spain

Fullback
Harry Shuford

Fullback
Bob Finley

Quarterback
Johnny Sprague

Guard
Billy Stamps

Tackle Maurice Orr

End
Maco
Stewart

TCU'S 1935 NATIONAL CHAMPIONS

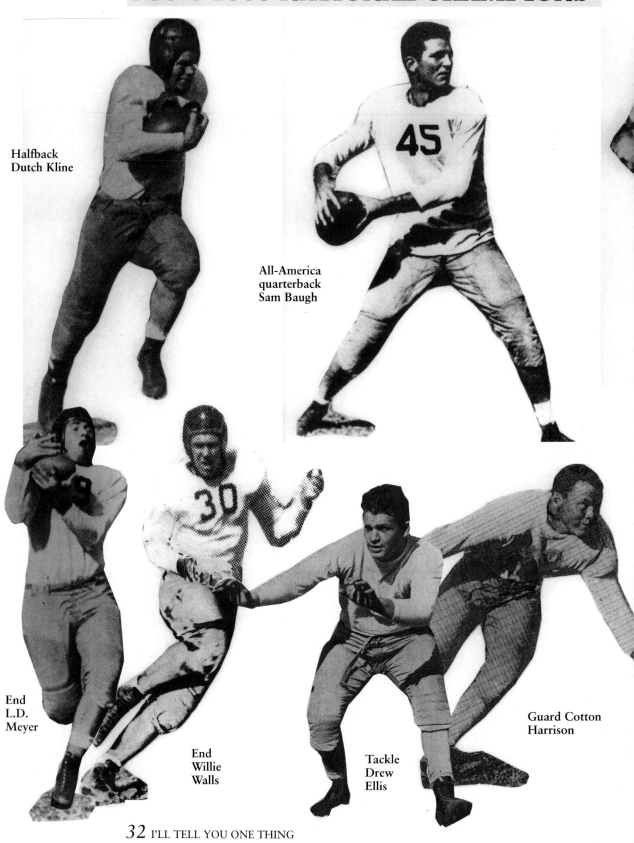

Halfback
Dutch Kline

All-America
quarterback
Sam Baugh

End
L.D.
Meyer

End
Willie
Walls

Tackle
Drew
Ellis

Guard Cotton
Harrison

Fullback
Tillie Manton

Halfback
Jimmy Lawrence

All-America
center
Darrell
Lester

Guard
Tracy
Kellow

Tackle
Wilson
Groseclose

End
Walter
Roach

FOUR

T.J. WAS asleep.

Actually, he was only pretending to be, his face buried in his folded arms on the bar, fake snoozing noises coming out of him.

Billy Clyde was on the stool next to T.J., reading the show biz section of *USA Today*, and shaking his head. He didn't recognize any of the names of the movie stars in the stories. But no big loss, he said. They were a pack of dippy 16-year-olds anyhow, and who cared about what movies they were in, other than people with their tongues pierced?

Tommy Earl was still over at the booth under the Humphrey Bogart and Ingrid Bergman poster talking to the shapely adorable in the too-tight, rump-high minidress. He'd gone over there to give her two hundred dollars to keep wearing that dress till the jewelry stores opened in the morning.

It was Tami Kay Mitchell, the rack-loaded wool-driver tending the bar, who nudged T.J. and said, "I think we're just about out of 1935."

"Really?" I said. "I was just getting ready to say what a shame it was that Bobby Wilson didn't win the Heisman in '35."

T.J. stirred slightly, faked another snooze noise.

Billy Clyde said, "Well, if you want to talk about heartbreak, what about me not winning it in '73?"

"At least you were eligible," I said.

"What's that mean?" Billy Clyde asked.

We were distracted momentarily, noticing that Tommy Earl had taken a seat next to the shapely adorable. He'd put his hand on her thigh, and started one of his monologues.

A good guess was, it would be the speech where he'd apologize for being born with a silver spoon in his mouth but point out how good things often came of it, such as the pleasure of contributing vast amounts of money to charity, and also being able to travel the world extensively and become better acquainted with the people and sights of so many fascinating places — Rome, Paris, London, the Alps, the Rhine, the Nile. And surely he'd mention what a lonely life it was, being single and all — and what color Porsche did she want?

Tami Kay said, "Looks like Tommy Earl's picked another Heisman winner. Last week he told me I won it."

"You've still got my two votes," Billy Clyde said playfully, nodding in the general direction of her lungs.

She said, "A married man's vote don't count."

"Wait a second," Billy Clyde said. "Tommy Earl's married."

"Not all of him," Tami Kay said.

Now Billy Clyde turned to me. "What's this about the Heisman?"

Bobby Wilson, I said. Bobby Wilson wasn't eligible for the first Heisman Trophy, and neither was Sam Baugh, or Wallace and McCauley at Rice, or Bobby

SMU's Bobby Wilson, "the Corsicana Comet"

Bobby Wilson explodes for a long run against Texas.

Grayson at Stanford — anybody decent who played west of the Mississippi River. It was an Eastern thing in the beginning, for the first year anyhow.

"Now I won't sleep at all tonight," Billy Clyde said.

The award that went to Jay Berwanger of the University of Chicago in '35 wasn't even called the Heisman by the Downtown Athletic Club of New York. It was called the Downtown Athletic Club Trophy.

Jay Berwanger probably got it because he was a good player on a weak team. He was known as "the One Man Gang." You couldn't really say that his teammates at the University of Chicago Maroons were a bunch of little scientists playing at football on their way to inventing the atomic bomb, but Chicago was only four years away from dropping the sport completely.

Here's the thing. Berwanger played only eight games in '35 and Chicago lost four of them, including three wipeouts. They lost to Nebraska by 28 to 7, to Indiana by 24 to 0, and to Purdue by 19 to 0. And the four games the Maroons won were over John Carroll — as in "Who?" — and Western State — as in "Gimme a break" — and by 13 to 7 over a Wisconsin team that finished 1-7, and by 7 to 6 over an Illinois team that went 3-5.

Meanwhile, Bobby Wilson was leading SMU to that national championship with 12 wins, not four, and one of those was the Poll Bowl victory

SOUTHERN METHODIST

ALL AMERICAN

BOB WILSON   *Halfback*

over TCU in which he was the superhero, both on the field and on coast-to-coast radio. But of course he was "the Corsicana Comet," the Mustangs' big play guy, all season long.

His '35 resume: he ran 36 and 22 yards for touchdowns in the North Texas State opener, spun off scoring runs of 49 and 34 yards against Tulsa, twisted 70 and 10 yards for touchdowns against Washington of Missouri, zigzagged 68 yards in the big Rice game — and four yards for the clinching touchdown — wiggled 38 yards for a touchdown against Hardin-Simmons, went 50 yards with a punt against Texas and scored once on a 12-yard sweep, turned into a passer against UCLA and set up two scores with his tosses, flipped a 35-yard touchdown pass in the Arkansas game, got off runs of 66 and 27 yards against Baylor, scoring once, and in the last game of the regular season before a home crowd in Ownby Stadium, he sparked the Mustangs over Texas A&M with a stirring 58-yard punt return for a touchdown.

Small wonder Grantland Rice called Wilson "the greatest running back of 1935."

But he wasn't eligible for the Heisman.

It seemed reasonable to assume that if the Heisman voters had been permitted to compare Bobby Wilson's season with Jay Berwanger's, it would have been your basic no contest.

To which Billy Clyde said, "But if you'd been old enough to vote and TCU had won that game over SMU, you'd have voted for Sam Baugh, wouldn't you?"

I didn't have to respond to that. T.J. raised his head up and said, "Is the Pope a bear?"

GREAT BACKS OF THE SWC

Johnny McCauley, Rice.

Kyle Gillespie, TCU's Orange Bowl quarterback in 1941.

TCU's Jimmy Lawrence.

A&M's Dick Todd, "the Crowell Cyclone," starred from 1936 through 1938.

TCU'S do-it-all Lindy Berry, All–America in 1949.

Texas All-Americans Jack Crain, 1941; Harrison Stafford, 1932; Bohn Hilliard, 1934.

Cy Leland, "the Lubbock Jackrabbit," TCU's first great running back in 1929 and 1930.

FIVE

TOMMY EARL BRUNER let the minidress slide. He came back to the bar and reported, "That little sumbitch over there's about as much fun as a plate of okra."

I took a stab at it. "She's in love with Tami Kay."

"Lot of that going around," said T.J., now fully awake.

Billy Clyde said, "Don't joke about it. You've got to be careful these days. Make a move on the wrong shapely, a skag in hiking boots might take it to DefCom 4 and kick you to death."

"Naw, it ain't that," said Tommy Earl. "She's waiting for some TV people. They're in town for the game tomorrow. A friend of hers knows one of the TV people. She heard the rumor they're coming in here with TV cameras. She thinks she might wind up in the movies. An I.Q. deal."

"Why's TV coming in here?" T.J. asked.

Tommy Earl said, "They're shooting 'local color.' Going all around town ... bars, restaurants, hangouts. Shooting stuff to throw in there with their blimp shots. Somebody told the network this was a real sports bar, not one of them places that looks like a Blackeyed Chili Tuesday's, everybody watching soccer and ice hockey, drinking Bud Lite, eating cheese sticks with their lottery numbers."

"I'm glad to know this is a sports bar," Tami Kay said. "Here I've been all these months thinking it was a homeless shelter."

If you gazed around the room, you could see a good enough supply of out-of-work guys in golf shirts to qualify He's Not Here as a sports bar.

"What's her name, the dumpling over there?" T.J. asked Tommy Earl as he studied the minidress in the booth.

Tommy Earl said, "I don't remember, something from the Erica family. She's dumber'n a hardwood floor."

"That didn't use to be an issue," Billy Clyde said.

"A man matures," Tommy Earl said. "I'll tell you what. I'd bet on Erica there to drill a hole through a stainless steel door. She's a hairstylist in one of those franchise barbershops. The Clip Joint ... Hair Today, Gone Tomorrow ... She works out there in one of those new suburbs nobody's ever seen and nobody can find but seven million people live there in three-story tract mansions. They got four SUVs, a swimming pool in the backyard, and a golf course on the other side of the lake where the water moccasins hold their bimonthly conventions."

"Creek Vista Ranchville," I said, helping out.

Tommy Earl said, "There you go. Only two Cracker Barrels and a Tom Thumb from the war of the malls. So ... she cuts this guy's hair the other day and he asks her to trim his eyebrows. She says she can't do that, she's not allowed to. The guy tells her he's been getting his hair cut and his eyebrows trimmed in that place for two years, and it's never been a problem. She says it's against the law to trim a man's eyebrows. That's what her manager told her. The guys says, okay, how 'bout this? I'll give you a $10 tip to trim my eyebrows. She says she's tempted, but she thinks about something, and says to the guy, well, if you're an undercover agent and I get arrested, $10 won't do me much good, will it? The guy gets hot, calls her a stupid fool, storms out. Don't even tip her nothin' for the haircut. But she's convinced she did the right thing, not breaking the law. Now, I just told y'all that story in half the time it took her to tell it to me. It took her so long I was too wore out to laugh at the idea of an undercover eyebrow agent."

Billy Clyde said, "I don't think she's boring at all. That's more interesting than anything else I've heard today."

I said, "Personal attacks don't faze a man who lives in the past."

T.J. said, "I wonder if Whoa Nellie will be one of them TV people coming in here?"

"Whoa Nellie keeps trying to retire," Billy Clyde said.

"What for?"

"What for? Why does he want to retire? I imagine he's tired of saying Whoa, Nellie. I know I'd be. Red Grange is who I miss. I grew up on Red Grange doing the Chicago Bears. Harlon Hill, he have the good hands. Eddie Brown have the good arm. Chicago have taken it down to the Green Bay end zone."

"Harlon Hill have the good hands?" Tommy Earl grinned.

"That's how Red said it. Red used to talk about Zupp on the air, too. His old coacher at Illinois, Bob Zuppke. Red remembered how Zupp would tell him to 'taken that foobaw' and let 'em see what Old Double Seven looks like from behind."

T.J. said, "I wouldn't be all that tickled about it if Frankenburger comes in here."

"Frankenstein Meets Musburger," Billy Clyde said.

"Musburger Meets Dracula," Tommy Earl added.

"Musburger Meets the Wolf Man," T.J. said.

Billy Clyde closed it out. "The Bride of Musburger Meets Florida State-Clemson."

My basic problem with college football on TV nowadays is the fact that they don't let you see or hear the bands anymore at halftime. You have to watch some girl announcer try to catch up with a coach headed for the dressing room so she can ask him if he's still happy to be an American. Then you get to be entertained by all the promos of sitcoms you wouldn't watch unless somebody pointed a gun at your head. After that, you get to see part scores and highlights of all the games you don't care about, and no score of the only game you're interested in.

"The Aggie band's never lost a halftime," I said, "and if they ever do, I'd like to be able to see it."

"Hullabaloo, caneck, caneck," T.J. muttered.

Tommy Earl sang: "Goodbye to Texas Uni ... ver-sity. Farewell to the Orange and the White. We are ... the good old Texas ... Aaa-ag-gies ..."

He stopped there and said, "World's greatest fight song, I've got to admit, even though I wouldn't pull an Aggie out of a ditch."

"Wrong," I said.

"Wrong what?"

He was told the "Aggie War Hymn" was a real good one, and ranked among the Top Ten Fight Songs, but it wasn't the best one.

"I got your best," Billy Clyde said, and made a semi-effort to sing, "Hail to the victors valiant, hail to the conquering heroes ... Hail, hail, to Mich-i-gan, the ..."

"Nope."

"... champions of the West. What do you mean nope?"

"It's in there," I said, "but not the best."

Billy Clyde frowned. "I sure hope you're not gonna say you think cheer, cheer, for old what's her name is the best."

Notre Dame was 10th, I revealed.

T.J. said, "When did you make this in-depth study of fight songs?"

"Shortly after cars came with tape decks.'

Then I elaborated on what constituted a good fight song. Essentially, it was a fight song that was rousing — met the goose-bump factor — and had a good melody along with it. And it couldn't be a cliche — like Notre Dame's, except Notre Dame's had a good tune, which saved it.

Your dull fight songs were things like "On Wisconsin," "Rambling Wreck," "Fight On USC," "Boomer Sooner." Get old quick. Too repetitive.

Tami Kay said, "Why don't you make a list of the best fight songs? I'll tack it up on the wall somewhere and people can throw darts at it. Something to entertain the customers."

Tommy Earl said, "I'd hang it in the men's room. That way if any Trojans or Sooners come in, they can do something else to it."

I made the list and said the only way anybody could disagree with it would be if they didn't like good tunes. It came out like this:

THE TEN BEST COLLEGE FIGHT SONGS

1. "Across the Field" — Ohio State
2. "The Victors" — Michigan
3. "Aggie War Hymn" — Texas A&M
4. "Go, Alabama" — Alabama
5. "Texas Taps" ('Texas Fight") — University of Texas
6. "Buckeye Battle Cry" — Ohio State
7. "Stanford Jonah" — California
8. "Hail to Georgia" — Georgia
9. "Fight for California" — California
10. "Victory March" — Notre Dame

There was some talk about Ohio State and California each having two fight songs in the Top Ten.

I said I couldn't help it, they were great songs, and a man of taste had no choice but to pick them. I also explained that it would have been remiss of me not to rank Ohio State's "Across the Field" No. 1 because it happened to be Paschal High's fight song as well.

"Set the air reverberating, so to speak," I said.

Several other fight songs came close to making the Top Ten. In no particular order, they were:

"Down the Field" (Yale), "Dear Old Nebraska U.," "Illinois Loyalty," "Go U. Northwestern," "Indiana Our Indiana," "Washington and Lee Swing," "Roar, Lion, Roar" (Columbia), "The Cannon Song" (Princeton), and "Love and Honor to Miami" (Miami of Ohio), which used to be "Wave the Flag for Old Chicago" in Jay Berwanger's day.

Of course the two best college football songs of all time are "You've Got to be a Football Hero" and "Mr. Touchdown, USA." They aren't fight songs for anybody, but they have splendid tunes and are good to hum on the way to the stadium on Saturdays.

Trying to decide on the best college fight songs wasn't all that difficult, I explained to my pals. All it required was turning up the stereo, grabbing an old Tommy Armour putter for a baton, and marching around in the garage for a couple of hours.

SIX

A MAN OF the college football persuasion is capable of talking for hours on the subject of why his game is better — more exciting, more interesting, more important — than any other team game, particularly those where the guys wear bloomers or ice skates or leotards, or that soccer thing where nobody ever falls on a loose ball.

I even take it up to another level and say that college football is vastly more entertaining than pro football. And for reasons that, if you laid them down, would stretch from the Stanford sorority girl in Palo Alto, California, shuffling a deck of daddy's credit cards, to the factory worker having a shot and beer in Buffalo, New York.

Here are the 10 reasons why you should love college football more than pro football, or almost anything else that people do standing up:

1. College fans can remember the great college games they won or lost better than they can the names of their aunts and uncles.

2. College teams don't relocate. The Michigan Wolverines are not going to move to St. Louis and become the St. Louis Wolverines, and the Oklahoma Sooners are not going to Tuscaloosa to become the Alabama Sooners because, well, for one reason, Alabama's not going to Oakland to become the Alabama Raiders.

3. College cheerleaders. They're real. They aren't dance bimbos, not that there's anything wrong with dance bimbos, other than the fact that they work for pro teams.

4. College teams have unique names. You know a Buckeye can't be in the NFL East, just as you know a Cornhusker can't be in the NFL West. The collegiate ranks are filled with originals. Only on their own campuses can you find Horned Frogs, Longhorns, Razorbacks, Boilermakers, Trojans, Volunteers, Gators, Seminoles, Badgers, Gophers, Hawkeyes, Mustangs, Tar Heels, Jayhawks, Wolverines, Rebels, Gamecocks, Blue Devils.

You see these things, you know what they are. Meanwhile, all you can say to a Giant is, "Gee, you look awfully small to be a giant." Or to a Jet, "Aren't you kind of fat to be a jet?" Or to a Brown, "What's a Brown?"

5. Most colleges have stadiums on the campus, most pro teams have stadiums in a tangle of freeways.

6. Most college towns have charm, atmosphere, leaf-lined boulevards. Most pro towns have picket lines outside the factory.

7. College games are affordable. A season ticket to a pro game costs more than a college education, and all you get to watch are holding calls.

8. College teams run a variety of offenses. Pro teams all look the same, except some teams drop more passes.

9. Tailgates. College tailgate parties are known for their candelabra, linens, silverware, cocktails, fine wines, potato salad sculpture, tossed salads, and New York strips.

Pro tailgate parties are known for their Bud Lites, link sausage, and complaints about heating costs.

10. Music. I've been over this, but colleges have great songs while pro teams have ... like, nothing. Zero, nada, the old Zippo lighter. You've never heard pro football fans sing:

"Go tell the Dolphins how to behave,

"Send the Dallas Cowboys to a watery grave."

Never. Doesn't happen.

There are numerous other reasons why the college game is better, but I won't go into them. Just let it be said that they have to do with live mascots, serious rivalries, marching bands, recognizable uniforms, homecoming queens — I'm married to one — pep rallies, bowl games, All-America teams, history, tradition, Heisman trophies, and no free agency.

☆

T.J. Lambert had a question. "If you don't like pro football, how come you write them books about it?"

"I'm appealing to the lowest common denominator," I explained.

"Common who? That's what you call me and Billy Clyde?"

"No, you're great Americans and wonderful human beings."

"You said something about a common deal."

"Denominators."

"I don't care what kind of refrigerators they own. I want to know who you're talkin' about."

"Pro football fans. They can't afford a sense of history. They're too busy worrying about what city their team will move to next year. Your lowest common denominators are people who don't know about Jim Thorpe kicking four field goals and running 70 yards for a touchdown to beat Harvard in 1911. They don't know about Centre College's Praying Colonels, and how Bo McMillin's 30-yard run beat Harvard in 1921. Ended a 25-game win streak. People who don't know about Army's Chris Cagle and Yale's Albie Booth — 'Little Boy Blue.' How they put on one of the great broken-field duels in '29. Cagle went 60 and 65 yards for touchdowns . . . Booth went for 70 and 75 yards for touchdowns. People who don't know about Alabama's great passing combination in '23 — Dixie Howell to Don Hutson. People who don't know about . . ."

"I got you," T.J. said. "You're talkin' about all them Lugi Bojacks. Mr. Intestine and Mr. Constipated."

"Right, Johnny Lujack . . . Glenn Davis and Doc Blanchard. Talking about 'The Game of the Century,' Notre Dame and Army at Yankee Stadium in '46. Lujack against Davis and Blanchard. All the great college games."

"You know about all the great college games?"

"Every one."

"Why you want to keep up with all that?"

"Because it's fun — and more interesting than trying to figure out whether Chipdip on the New York Exchange is gonna go from five and three-eighths to six and two-thirds. Want to know what the 50 greatest college games of the 20th century were?"

T.J. asked Billy Clyde if he wanted to know.

"Do I have a choice?" Billy Clyde said.

I smiled and said, "It won't take that long. I will just run out the car and get my charts and easel."

COLLEGE FOOTBALL'S 50 GREATEST GAMES OF THE 20TH CENTURY

DATE, SITE	OPPONENTS	TOP PLAYERS	RESULT
Nov. 23, 1905 Chicago	Michigan (12-0) vs. Chicago (9-0)	Germany Schultz, c Walter Eckersall, qb	2-0, Chicago
Nov. 11, 1911 Cambridge	Carlisle (8-0) vs. Harvard (5-1)	Jim Thorpe, fb Percy Wendell, hb	18-15, Carlisle
Nov. 16, 1920 West Point	Notre Dame (4-0) vs. Army (5-0)	George Gipp, fb Gar Davidson, t	27-17, Notre Dame
Oct. 29, 1921 Cambridge	Harvard (5-0-1) vs. Centre (7-0)	John Brown, g Bo McMillin, hb	6-0, Centre

Oct. 29, 1922 Chicago	Princeton (4-0) vs. Chicago (5-0)	Herb Treat, t John Thomas, hb	20-18, Princeton
Jan. 1, 1925 Rose Bowl	Notre Dame (9-0) vs. Stanford (7-0-1)	"Four Horsemen" Ernie Nevers, fb	27-10, Notre Dame
Nov. 27, 1926 Chicago	Navy (9-0) vs. Army (7-1)	Tom Hamilton, hb Chris Cagle, hb	21-21, Tie
Oct. 29, 1929 West Point	Yale (2-1) vs. Army (3-0-1)	Albie Booth, hb Chris Cagle, hb	21-13 Yale
Nov. 16, 1929 Chicago	Notre Dame (6-0) vs. USC (6-1)	Frank Carideo, qb Russ Saunders, hb	13-12 Notre Dame
Nov. 23, 1931 South Bend	Notre Dame (6-0-1) vs. USC (6-1)	Marchy Schwartz, hb Shaver, Mohler, Pinckert	16-14, USC
Jan. 1, 1934 Rose Bowl	Stanford (8-1-1) vs. Columbia (7-1)	Bobby Grayson, hb. Cliff Montgomery, qb	7-0, Columbia
Oct. 20, 1934 Pittsburgh	Minnesota (2-0) vs. Pittsburgh (3-0)	Pug Lund, hb Izzy Weinstock, fb	13-7, Minnesota
Jan. 1, 1935 Rose Bowl	Alabama (9-0) vs. Stanford (9-0-1)	Dixie Howell to Don Hutson Bobby Grayson fb	19-13, Alabama
Nov. 2, 1935 Columbia, O.	Notre Dame (5-0) vs. Ohio State (4-0)	Bill Shakespeare, qb Tippy Dye, qb	18-13, Notre Dame
Nov. 30, 1935 Fort Worth	TCU (10-0) vs. SMU (10-0)	Sam Baugh, qb Bobby Wilson, hb	20-14, SMU
Oct. 16, 1937 New York City	Pittsburgh (3-0) vs. Fordham (3-0)	Marshall Goldberg, hb "Seven Blocks of Granite"	0-0, Tie
Jan. 2, 1939 Sugar Bowl	TCU (10-0) vs. Carnegie Tech (7-1)	Davey O'Brien, qb George Muha, hb	15-7, TCU
Jan. 1, 1940 Rose Bowl	Tennessee (10-0) vs. USC (7-0-2)	George Cafego, hb Grenny Lansdell, qb	14-0, USC
Nov. 9, 1940 Dallas	Texas A&M (6-0) vs. SMU (4-0-1)	John Kimbrough, fb Ray Mallouf, qb	19-7, Texas A&M
Nov. 9, 1940 Minneapolis	Michigan (5-0) vs. Minnesota (5-0)	Tom Harmon, hb Bruce Smith, hb	7-6, Minnesota

Oct. 31, 1942 Atlanta	Georgia (6-0) vs. Alabama (5-0)	Frank Sinkwich, qb Russ Craft, hb	20-10, Georgia
Nov. 9, 1946 New York City	Notre Dame (5-0) vs. Army (7-0)	Johnny Lujack, qb Davis & Blanchard	0-0, Tie
Nov. 1, 1947 Dallas	SMU (5-0) vs. Texas (6-0)	Doak Walker, hb Bobby Layne, qb	14-13, SMU
Nov. 29, 1947 Fort Worth	SMU (9-0) vs. TCU (4-4-1)	Doak Walker, hb Lindy Berry	19-19, Tie
Dec. 3, 1949 Dallas	Notre Dame (9-0) vs. SMU (5-3-1)	Emil Sitko, hb Kyle Rote, hb	27-20, Notre Dame
Nov. 25, 1950 Norman, Okla.	Oklahoma (8-0) vs. Nebraska (6-1-1)	Billy Vessels, hb Bobby Reynolds, hb	49-35, Oklahoma
Oct. 20, 1951 Berkeley	USC (4-0) vs. California (4-0)	Frank Gifford, hb Johnny Olszewski, fb	21-14, USC
Jan. 2, 1956 Orange Bowl	Oklahoma (10-0) vs. Maryland (10-0)	Tommy McDonald, hb Eddie Vereb, hb	20-6, Oklahoma
Oct. 20, 1956 College Station	TCU (3-0) vs. Texas A&M (3-0-1)	Jim Swink, hb John David Crow, hb	7-6, TexasA&M
Nov. 16, 1957 Norman, Okla.	Oklahoma (7-0) vs. Notre Dame (4-2)	Clendon Thomas, hb Nick Petrosante, fb	7-0, Notre Dame
Oct. 31, 1959 Baton Rouge	LSU (6-0) vs. Ole Miss (6-0)	Billy Cannon, hb Jake Gibbs, qb	7-3, LSU
Jan. 1, 1963 Rose Bowl	USC (10-0) vs. Wisconsin (8-1)	Pete Beathard, qb Ron VanderKelen, qb	42-37, UCS
Jan. 1, 1965 Orange Bowl	Alabama (10-0) vs. Texas (9-1)	Joe Namath, qb Tommy Nobis, g-lb	21-17, Texas
Nov. 19, 1966 East Lansing	Notre Dame (8-0) vs. Michigan State (9-0)	Coley O'Brien, qb Bubba Smith, de	10-10, Tie
Nov. 18, 1967 Los Angeles	UCLA (8-0-1) vs. USC (8-1)	Gary Beban, qb O.J. Simpson, hb	21-20, USC

Oct. 4, 1969 Birmingham	Alabama (2-0) vs. Ole Miss (1-1)	Scott Hunter, qb Archie Manning, qb	33-32, Alabama
Dec. 6, 1969 Fayetteville	Texas (9-0) vs. Arkansas (9-0)	James Street, qb Bill Montgomery, qb	15-14, Texas
Nov. 20, 1971 Norman	Nebraska (10-0) vs. Oklahoma (9-0)	Johnny Rodgers, hb Jack Mildren, qb	35-31, Nebraska
Jan. 1, 1974 Sugar Bowl	Alabama (11-0) vs. Notre Dame (11-0)	Richard Todd, qb Tom Clements, qb	24-23, Notre Dame
Jan. 1, 1975 Rose Bowl	USC (9-1-1) vs. Ohio State (10-1)	Pat Haden, qb Archie Griffin, hb	18-17, USC
Nov. 8, 1980 Jacksonville	Georgia (8-0) vs. Florida (6-1)	Herschel Walker, hb Wayne Peace, qb	26-21, Georgia
Jan. 1, 1983 Sugar Bowl	Georgia (10-1) vs. Penn State (10-1)	Herschel Walker, hb Todd Blackledge, qb	27-23, Penn State
Jan. 1, 1984 Orange Bowl	Nebraska (12-0) vs. Miami (10-1)	Turner Gill, qb Bernie Kosar, qb	31-30, Miami
Nov. 24, 1984 Miami	Boston College (9-2) vs. Miami (8-3)	Doug Flutie, qb Bernie Kosar, qb	47-45, B.C.
Oct. 3, 1987 Tallahassee	Miami (2-0) vs. Florida State (4-0)	Michael Irvin, e Danny McManus, qb	26-25, Miami
Oct. 15, 1988 South Bend	Miami (4-0) vs. Notre Dame (5-0)	Steve Walsh, qb Tony Rice, qb	31-30, Notre Dame
Jan. 1, 1991 Orange Bowl	Colorado (11-1-1) vs. Notre Dame (9-2)	Eric Bieniemy, hb Rocket Ismail, rec.	10-9, Colorado
Nov. 26, 1993 Tallahassee	Florida State (11-1) vs. Florida (10-1)	Charlie Ward, qb Errict Rhett, hb	33-21, Florida State
Nov. 22, 1997 Gainesville	Florida State (10-0) vs. Florida (8-2)	Peter Warrick, rec. Jacquez Green, rec.	32-29, Florida
Jan. 1, 1998 Rose Bowl	Michigan (11-0) vs. Washington State (10-1)	Brian Griese, qb Ryan Leaf, qb	21-16, Michigan

SEVEN

"**S**EEN YOUR share of Poll Bowls, haven't you, old-timer?"

Wise-mouth from Billy Clyde.

Except it happened to be true. Me and Poll Bowls have been an item for years. After I was lucky enough to see a few as a kid, I was lucky enough to cover a few as a grownup.

A true Poll Bowl, in case you don't know, is a game that matches undefeated teams for high stakes at some point after the season's under way.

They weren't called Poll Bowls until later years, they were just known as big games in the blossoming days of the Southwest Conference. The material was pretty well balanced for what Kern Tips called the "family squabbles," and every team tried to line up exotic intersectional opponents on the road. It was a way to make more money for the athletic budget. Those two things combined to make it difficult for somebody to scrape through a season with no losses.

Southwest Conference teams went on the road to meet Santa Clara (near San Francisco), Fordham, NYU, and Manhattan College in New York City, USC and UCLA in L.A., Temple in Philadelphia, and Ohio State in Columbus. All those along with Notre Dame, Navy, Pittsburgh, Minnesota, Wisconsin, Villanova, Colorado, Kansas, Ole Miss, North Carolina, Nebraska, LSU, and Tulane — even such eccentric foes as the Detroit U. Titans, the Washington U. Bears in St. Louis, the St. Mary's Galloping Gaels in Oakland, the George Washington Colonials in Washington, D.C., the Duquesne Night Riders in Pittsburgh, and the Creighton Bluejays in Omaha.

Teams traveled by passenger train in that romantic era and frequently took two and three days to reach the game — sometimes with the band, cheerleaders, and fans on board.

There'd be a sportswriter on board, too, and on the way to Philadelphia he'd be asked to file a story, and one of them might say, "TCU's special train stopped last night so the Frogs could practice offense and defense. They worked out on a high school field near, I think, Dayton, Ohio."

The next big-deal Poll Bowl that presented itself to the conference — the kind that made people say they'd eat dirty laundry for a ticket — was between TCU and Baylor. It occurred on a Saturday afternoon in the middle of the 1938 season, and once again the game was in Fort Worth.

That was the year TCU did it all.

The Frogs' modest little Davey O'Brien, only 5-8 and 155 pounds, became the unanimous All-America quarterback of 1938 and the first player to win the Heisman, Maxwell, and Walter Camp awards all in the same season as the game's outstanding player.

O'Brien won those awards over such other All-Americans as Columbia's Sid Luckman, Pitt's Marshall Goldberg, and Tennessee's George Cafego by leading the nation in passing and total offense as he carried TCU to a perfect 10-0 season and the clear-cut national championship in both the AP and Williamson rankings. Afterward came the thrilling Sugar Bowl victory over Carnegie Tech, the best team in the East.

"Slingshot" Davey O'Brien, TCU's Heisman, Maxwell and Camp winner in 1938, the year he led the nation in passing and total offense.

The Frogs were imposing enough that two of their linemen made All-America along with O'Brien — center Ki Aldrich and tackle I.B. Hale — and an unheard-of eight out of eleven Frogs made all-conference.

The '38 Frogs were being called a great ball club even before the Poll Bowl with Baylor.

Up in Philadelphia against Pop Warner's Temple team, O'Brien had fired perfect touchdown strikes of 49, 30, and 56 yards in the 28 to 6 victory, and the gray-thatched Pop Warner said, "That Davey O'Brien is the greatest passer I've ever looked at, and I've been looking a long time."

A week later O'Brien hurled three more touchdown passes as TCU beat Texas A&M 34 to 6 — crushing an A&M team that was only a year away from being a national champion itself — and Aggie Coach Homer Norton said, "TCU has the greatest team I've ever seen on the field."

Baylor was as undefeated as TCU after five games when they collided on the warm, dry Saturday of October 29, 1938, and it had already been established for mankind that they were not only the two top teams in the conference, they were among the best in the country.

Davey O'Brien faced a nifty quarterback in his own right, a wiry, versatile guy known to Texas sportswriters as "Bullet Bill" Patterson, "the Hillsboro Home-Run Hitter." Such writing, huh?

In TCU Stadium the crowd was a brimming-over 30,000, and my uncle and I were among those packed into the grassy slope of the north end zone, but that turned out to be a good spot — most of the touchdowns were scored right in front of us.

The lineups at the kickoff:

TCU		BAYLOR
Don Looney	LE	Sam Boyd
I.B. Hale	LT	Frank Marx
Forrest Kline	LG	Leonard Akin
Ki Aldrich	C	Robert Nelson
Bud Taylor	RG	Bobby Taylor
Allie White	RT	Bennett Edwards
Durward Horner	RE	Sherman Barnes
Davey O'Brien	QB	Billy Patterson
Earl Clark	LH	Ted Lewellyn
Johnny Hall	RH	Fred Graham
Connie Sparks	FB	Milt Merka

By now I was a mature 10-year-old who'd learned not to be too impressed by the uniforms of visiting teams, yet Baylor's were something to behold — green and gold from hat to knee. Gold shoulders and gold numerals on the green jerseys, and

National Champions from the Southwest Conference
(Selected by everybody from the AP to some guy you've probably never heard of.)

TEXAS A&M, 1919
RECORD: 10-0
Selector: National Championship Foundation*
COACH: Dana X. Bible
STAR PLAYERS: fullback Jack Mahan, halfback Roswell Higginbotham, guard Cap Murrah, end Scott Alexander, guard E.S. Wilson
POSTSEASON: no bowl available
(* A predated selection of the NCF, named in 1980.)

SMU, 1935
RECORD: 12-1
Selectors: Dickinson System, Houlgate System
COACH: Matty Bell
STAR PLAYERS: halfback Bobby Wilson, guard J.C. (Ironman) Wetsel, tackle Truman Spain, fullback Harry Shuford
POSTSEASON: lost Rose Bowl to No. 5 Stanford, 7-0

TCU, 1935
RECORD: 12-1
Selectors: Williamson Rankings, Maxwell Survey
COACH: Dutch Meyer
STAR PLAYERS: quarterback Sam Baugh, halfback Jimmy Lawrence, center Darrell Lester, end Walter Roach
POSTSEASON: Won Sugar Bowl over No. 3 LSU, 3-2

TCU, 1938
RECORD: 11-0
Selectors: AP, Williamson Rankings, Helms Athletic Foundation, National Championship Foundation*
COACH: Dutch Meyer
STAR PLAYERS: quarterback Davey O'Brien, tackle I.B. Hale, center Ki Aldrich, halfback Earl Clark, fullback Connie Sparks, end Don Looney
POSTSEASON: Won Sugar Bowl over No. 5 Carnegie Tech, 15-7
(* A predated selection of the NCF, named in 1980.)

TEXAS A&M, 1939
RECORD: 11-0
Selectors: AP, Williamson, Helms, Dunkel, Houlgate, Poling, *Illustrated Football Annual*, DeVold*, Billingsley*, Football Research Foundation*, National Championship Foundation*
COACH: Homer Norton
STAR PLAYERS: fullback John Kimbrough, halfback Jimmy Thomason, halfback Derace Moser, tackle Joe Boyd, guard Marshall Robnett
POSTSEASON: Won Sugar Bowl over No. 5 Tulane, 14-13
(* Billingsley, DeVold, Football Research, and NCF are all predated selections.)

TEXAS, 1941
RECORD: 8-1-1
Selectors: Williamson rankings, Berryman System*
COACH: Dana X. Bible
STAR PLAYERS: halfback Jack Crain, tailback Pete Layden, guard Chal Daniel, end Mal Kutner.
POSTSEASON: Turned down bid to Orange Bowl
(* A predated selection by Berryman, named in 1990.)

TEXAS, 1961
RECORD: 10-1
Selectors: Sagarin System*
COACH: Darrell Royal
STAR PLAYERS: halfback James Saxton, quarterback Mike Cotton, tackle Don Talbert, guard Johnny Treadwell
POSTSEASON: Won Cotton Bowl over No. 5 Ole Miss, 12-7
(* A predated selection by Sagarin, named in 1978.)

TEXAS, 1963
RECORD: 11-0
Selectors: AP, UPI, *Football Writers*, Williamson, Helms, Hall of Fame, Dunkel, Litkenhous, DeVold, Poling, *Football News*, Billingsley*, Berryman*, Football Research*, National Championship Foundation*, Sagarin*
COACH: Darrell Royal
STAR PLAYERS: quarterback Duke Carlisle, halfback Tommy Ford, tackle Scott Appleton, guard Tommy Nobis

POSTSEASON: Won Cotton Bowl over No. 2
Navy, 28-6
(* Predated selections.)

ARKANSAS, 1964
RECORD: 11-0
Selectors: *Football Writers*, Helms, Poling,
Billingsley*, Football Research*, National
Championship Foundation*
COACH: Frank Broyles
STAR PLAYERS: quarterback Fred Marshall,
fullback Bobby Burnett, tackle Lloyd Phillips,
end Jerry Lamb, defensive back Ken Hatfield
POSTSEASON: Won Cotton Bowl over No. 6
Nebraska, 10-7
(* Predated selections.)

TEXAS, 1968
RECORD: 9-1-1
Selectors: DeVold, Matthews, Sagarin*
COACH: Darrell Royal
STAR PLAYERS: quarterback James Street,
halfback Chris Gilbert, fullback Steve Worster,
end Deryl Comer, tackle Loyd Wainscott
POSTSEASON: Won Cotton Bowl over No. 7
Tennessee, 36-13
(* A predated selection by Sagarin, named in
1978.)

TEXAS, 1969
RECORD: 11-0
Selectors: AP, UPI, *Football Writers*, Helms,
Dunkel, *Football News*, Litkenhous, DeVold,
Hall of Fame, Poling, F.A.C.T. (Foundation
for Analysis of Competitions), Billingsley*,
Berryman*, Football Research*, Sagarin*,
National Championship Foundation*
COACH: Darrell Royal
STAR PLAYERS: quarterback James Street,
fullback Steve Worster, tackle Bob McKay,
end Cotton Speyrer, linebacker Glen Halsell
POSTSEASON: Won Cotton Bowl over No. 5
Notre Dame, 21-17
(* Predated selections.)

TEXAS, 1970
RECORD: 10-1
Selectors: UPI, Hall of Fame, Litkenhous,
F.A.C.T., Berryman*
COACH: Darrell Royal
STAR PLAYERS: quarterback Eddie Phillips,
fullback Steve Worster, halfback Jim Bertelsen,
end Cotton Speyrer, def. end Bill Atessis
POSTSEASON: Lost Cotton Bowl to No. 8
Notre Dame, 24-11
(* Predated selections.)

TEXAS, 1977
RECORD: 11-1
Selectors: F.A.C.T., Berryman*
COACH: Fred Akers
STAR PLAYERS: fullback Earl Campbell,
tackle Brad Shearer, end Johnny (Lam) Jones,
quarterback Rob Moerschal
POSTSEASON: Lost Cotton Bowl to No. 3
Notre Dame, 38-10
(* Predated selection.)

ARKANSAS, 1977
RECORD: 11-1
Selectors: F.A.C.T.
COACH: Lou Holtz
STAR PLAYERS: quarterback Ron Calcagni,
fullback Ben Cowins, guard Leotis Harris,
halfback Roland Sales.
POSTSEASON: Won Orange Bowl over No.
2 Oklahoma, 31-6

SMU, 1981
RECORD: 10-1
Selector: National Championship Foundation
COACH: Ron Meyer
STAR PLAYERS: halfback Eric Dickerson,
halfback Craig James, quarterback Lance
McIlhenny, def. lineman Harvey Armstrong
POSTSEASON: Ineligible for bowl due to
NCAA probation

TEXAS, 1981
RECORD: 10-1-1
Selector: National Championship Foundation
COACH: Fred Akers
STAR PLAYERS: quarterback Rick McIvor,
fullback A.J. (Jam) Jones, halfback John
Walker, tackle Kenneth Sims
POSTSEASON: Won Cotton Bowl over No. 6
Alabama, 14-12

SMU, 1982
RECORD: 11-0-1
Selector: Helms Athletic Foundation
COACH: Bobby Collins
STAR PLAYERS: halfback Eric Dickerson,
halfback Craig James, quarterback Lance
McIlhenny, def. back Russell Carter
POSTSEASON: Won Cotton Bowl over No. 7
Pittsburgh, 7-3

green stripes going up the gold pants in back and crossing over the gold helmet. Drum major attire, my uncle said.

What was more dazzling was TCU's attack. All kinds of spins and reverses and passes, and laterals coming off the pass catches, and laterals coming at the end of Davey O'Brien's squirts through the line. Magic.

The first half was filled with big plays and it ended with TCU ahead by only 13 to 7, and with Patterson and the Bears threatening on the Frogs' 8-yard line. But that was it. The second half was all Frogs. O'Brien flipped three touchdown passes again, and halfback Earl Clark turned into some kind of long-distance runner, and TCU buried Baylor by 39 to 7.

Here now to tell about it is a man who'd one day be the editor of a Dallas paper I labored for, but this was from his wire-service days:

By FELIX R. McKNIGHT

Associated Press Sports Writer

FORT WORTH, Oct. 29 — Mighty Texas Christian rustled up 524 yards by ground and air to rumble on undefeated with a 39-7 submersion of hitherto unbeaten Baylor before 30,000 Christian converts Saturday.

Icily calm about the whole thing, the Christians — perhaps the greatest of all Southwest Conference teams to date — stabbed the Baylor wall with runs that netted 288 yards and added 236 more with Slingshot Davey O'Brien's passing arm.

A little unsteady at the start, and ahead by only 13-7 at the half, the Christians blew the top off the game in the final two periods with incredible power and finesse.

Sophomore fullback Connie Sparks plunged for three touchdowns and Earl Clark, a wiggling broken-field marvel, scored two.

O'Brien, the 150-pound passing demon, loosed his tosses for three touchdowns and 236 yards out of 10 completions in 17 attempts.

For the first time in his three-year career, O'Brien momentarily went down with an injury in the third period, from a terrific blow by Baylor's All-America end, Sam Boyd. O'Brien shook off the injury, however. He re-entered the game and threw two more touchdown passes.

The Christians' victory was so brutally complete, it was said that Joe College, Baylor's 700-pound grizzly mascot, should be happy he was able to stay in his cage and didn't have to go out on the field. He might have wound up a rug.

In the context of today, you have to be amazed by TCU's showing at the polls in '38. Three big-name schools also finished undefeated and untied that year, but they were defeated handily by the Frogs in the rankings.

TCU's all-America center, Ki Aldrich (48) and tackle I.B. Hale (22) clear the way for halfback Johnny Hall in Baylor game.

TCU's great halfback Earl Clark dives for a score against Baylor in 1938 "Poll Bowl."

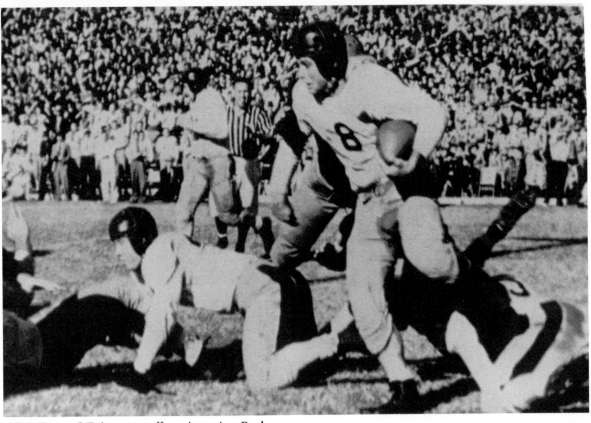

TCU's Davey O'Brien steps off a gain against Baylor.

The records of the top four teams in '38:

TCU, No. 1			TENNESSEE, No. 2		
13	Centenary	0	26	Sewanee	0
21	Arkansas	14	20	Clemson	7
28	Temple	6	7	Auburn	0
34	Texas A&M	6	13	Alabama	0
21	Marquette	0	44	The Citadel	0
39	Baylor	7	14	LSU	6
21	Tulsa	0	45	Chattanooga	0
28	Texas	6	14	Vanderbilt	0
29	Rice	7	46	Kentucky	0
20	SMU	7	47	Ole Miss	0

DUKE, No. 3			OKLAHOMA, No. 4		
18	VPI	0	7	Rice	6
27	Davidson	0	13	Texas	0
7	Colgate	0	19	Kansas	0
6	Georgia Tech	0	14	Nebraska	0
7	Wake Forest	0	28	Tulsa	6
14	North Carolina	0	26	Kansas State	0
21	Syracuse	0	21	Missouri	0
7	NC State	0	10	Iowa State	0
7	Pittsburgh	0	19	Oklahoma A&M	0
			28	Washington State	0

"Bullet Bill" Patterson, "the Hillsboro Home-Run Hitter." One of Baylor's greatest backs, he became MVP of the East-West Shrine game after the 1938 season.

There were reasons why TCU ran so well in the polls back then. For one thing, the Frogs hadn't been idle since the great season of '35. The following year, 1936, Sam Baugh again led the nation in passing and punting, and TCU wound up an 8-2-2 regular season by going out to San Francisco and upsetting Santa Clara 9 to 0. That was big news because the Broncos had gone into the game with a record of 8-0 — they were the only unbeaten, untied team left in the country and were ranked No. 1 by Williamson.

The two-time All-America Baugh and his Frogs were then invited to be the host team in the inaugural Cotton Bowl. There they met and defeated a highly-ranked Marquette team, 16 to 6, as Slingin' Sam out-slung the Golden Avalanche's own All-America tailback, Raymond (Buzz) Buivid.

The season of '37 helped things, too. O'Brien replaced Baugh that year and all he did was cause a near-panic in New York City when his touchdown pass to Don Looney led the unbeaten Fordham Rams and their "Seven Blocks of Granite" for 57 minutes before the Frogs bowed, 7 to 6. Later in the season Davey engineered the drive that upset the conference champion Rice Owls and their new set of "Touch-down Twins," Ernie Lain and Ollie Cordill, by the count of 7 to 2.

O'Brien, Aldrich, and Hale each made at least one All-America team in '37, so the sports world was famil-iar with TCU a year later.

The only prize that escaped TCU in '38 was the Rose Bowl bid. The Frogs were seriously considered, and got all excited, but the

---

The Autumn Thing

It's the day of the big game — huge — and I'm there to cover it.

I'm a campus collector. I've never met one I didn't like. So I start with a stroll around the campus. I admire the quad, the drag, the statues, the fountains, the architecture. I wonder what it would have been like to go to school here. This bench under these trees. Is this where I would have sat and smoked and drunk coffee so often? And maybe I can hear one of the bands rehearsing in the distance.

An hour before game time and I'm up on the out-door photo deck of the press box. I want to watch the stadium fill up, the teams warm up. I want to hear it, smell it, absorb it.

Minutes before the kickoff now. Both bands are blaring. Both sides of the stadium are fraught with nerves and noise. Both teams are on the sidelines, totally pumped, hopping about like speed freaks.

Seconds till the kickoff now, and the lineups are on the field — ready, wired, poised, game-faced. The entire crowd is making one continuous roar. The bell is about to ring for the opening round of a heavy-weight championship fight. The gun is up for the 100-meter dash in the Olympics. The Derby horses are in the gate at Churchill Downs. The cars are whining for the start at Indy.

But here in this college football stadium, this is my favorite moment in sports. Half of these thousands of fans will be deliriously happy tonight, the other half will live with a heartbreaking loss for the rest of their lives.

Upstairs in the press box, I'm even standing up.

— the Author

"Touchdown Twins" at Rice from 1937 to 1939, Ernie Lain (66) and Ollie Cordill (70).

invitation finally went to Duke, primarily because Wallace Wade, the Blue Devils' coach, lied. He guaranteed the selectors that his Duke team was far superior to the two Alabama teams he'd taken to Pasadena in the middle 1920s. So Duke went and promptly lost to a twice-beaten Southern Cal team, 7 to 3.

No. 1 TCU and No. 5 Carnegie Tech were invited to the Sugar Bowl, which left the Orange Bowl with Tennessee against Oklahoma. The result of these matchups was that TCU-Carnegie Tech turned out to be a jewel while Miami's fans saw a dud — the Sooners turned up badly crippled and Tennessee won easily, 17 to 0.

About the Carnegie Tech Tartans. They weren't a bunch of little boys in smocks lateraling test tubes and drop-kicking slide rules. They were tough, talented, beefy dudes in red jerseys and gold helmets, a powerful outfit with two great backs in George Muha and Merlin Condit. They came to New Orleans with a record of 7-1, and their one loss was a debatable 7-to-0 thing with Notre Dame.

In Carnegie Tech's game with the Irish, the zebras made two mistakes. One, they gave Notre Dame a "fifth down" to sustain a crucial series, and two, their "forgotten down" incident stopped a crucial Carnegie Tech drive. The Tartans screamed and hollered that the idiot zebras had cost them the game, but all Notre Dame said was "tough luck."

Contrast that with what Cornell did two years later. An unbeaten Cornell eleven, coached by Carl Snavely and led by halfback Walter (Pop) Scholl, had beaten all nine opponents in 1939 and all six opponents in 1940 and was ranked No. 1 in the nation when they ran into a mediocre but inspired Dartmouth team in their next-to-last game of the season. Trailing upstart Dartmouth 3 to 0 with time running out, Cornell mounted a drive and scored with only three seconds left to win, 7 to 3, and remain No. 1.

Except . . . another idiot zebra had given Cornell a "fifth down," and it was on that play that the Big Red scored with a five-yard pass into the end zone. Cornell's fourth-down pass had been incomplete, which should have ended the game.

But suddenly the wild Dartmouth celebration had quickly turned into a nightmare because of referee Red Friesell's mathematics, Red Friesell entering his name into football legend alongside Wrong Way Roy Riegels.

Ten days later, however, after viewing the film, Cornell admitted Red Friesell had made a ghastly mistake and refused to accept the win, and the game has long since been properly recorded as a 3-to-0 Dartmouth victory.

The sporting gentlemen at Notre Dame still claim a 7-to-0 victory over Carnegie Tech in 1938. Done deal.

The Tartans gave the Frogs a severe test in the Sugar Bowl. Davey O'Brien's shovel passes drove TCU to a 6-to-0 lead, but the Tartans scored on a 44-yard pass just before the half ended and led 7 to 6. It was the first time the national champion Frogs had trailed anyone all season, and up in the TCU cheering section at halftime, "strong men in Stetsons wept," according to a *Star-Telegram* sidebar.

Not to worry. Quickly in the third quarter O'Brien drove TCU 80 yards to a touchdown, the score coming on a 45-yard pass to the end, Durward Homer. In the fourth period, after stopping a Carnegie Tech threat, TCU iced the game away after another long drive when Davey kicked a 20-yard field goal to make the final score 15 to 7.

TCU Coach Dutch Meyer called it "the most exciting game I've ever seen — even better than the SMU game in '35."

If you bled purple in the Sugar Bowl stadium or by the radio back home in Forth Worth, you could only agree.

1938 TCU NATIONAL CHAMPIONS

Halfback Johnny Hall

Fullback Connie Sparks

End Durward Horner

Tackle Allie White

Guard Bud Taylor

All-America quarterback
Davey O'Brien

Halfback Earl Clark

All-America center
Ki Aldrich

Guard
Forrest Kline

All-America
tackle L.B. Hale

End Don Looney

SUGAR BOWL ACTION AS TCU WHIPS THE "BEST OF THE EAST"

Horned Frogs halfback Johnny Hall sweeps Carnegie Tech end.

Connie Sparks is under Tartans' pile for a touchdown.

TCU's Davey O'Brien zips through the Carnegie Tech defense.

EIGHT

GGIE JOKES don't do it for me.

I've always thought they'd be funnier if they were told about Harvard men. That's because I've always had a generous respect for Texas Aggies — they used to go off to war and do *Saving Private Ryan* things for us — while I've hardly ever met a Harvard man who could find the elevator.

So how many Harvard men does it take to change a lightbulb?

Six. Two to find the lightbulb, two to figure out which end goes where, and two to discuss its use in helping us become a more diversified and multicultural society.

And while I'm at it, why did the Harvard man choke to death in the restaurant after a dinner with friends? He had to pay the check, for once.

But back to the Texas Aggies, specifically those of 1939. They did a rare thing for the old Southwest Conference. They followed the TCU Horned Frogs as an undefeated, untied team, a Sugar Bowl winner, and the national champions.

This was the "John Kimbrough team," as it's mostly remembered, Jarrin' John having been Texas A&M's all-time biggest star. He was a tall, lumbering All-American fullback, a man who uncomfortably found himself compared to Bronko Nagurski in the pile-driving, line-wrecking department.

These Aggies are also remembered for their stingy defense. As they bludgeoned their way to a 10-0 record, they held their foes to a measly 1.71 yards gained per play — an NCAA record that still stands.

On offense they traveled mostly by ground. Out of Homer Norton's off-brand versions of the single-wing and spread-end formations, Kimbrough would plow through holes opened up by Joe Boyd, the All-America tackle, Marshall Robnett, the future All-America guard, and Jimmy Thomason, who's still regarded as one of the most vicious blocking backs that ever wore a leather helmet. Some broken-field tap dances would be added by the alternating wingbacks, Derace Moser and Bill Conatser. And guiding the offense, offering up a surprise pass now and then, were two capable quarterbacks. The primary signal-caller was a junior, Marion (Dookie) Pugh, a former Fort Worth high school star, but Walemon (Cotton) Price, the senior, played a larger role than most understudies.

The '39 Aggies were never confronted with a Poll Bowl, but there was an intersectional game of special significance early in the season on October 14 in Tyler, Texas, of all places.

That day as a special attraction of the annual "Tyler Rose Festival," the Texas Aggies took on a celebrated Eastern opponent, Villanova, which was rumbling along with a 21-game win streak. The Wildcats of Coach Clipper Smith hadn't lost a game since 1936.

Texas A&M's "Jarrin' John" Kimbrough, a two-time All-America fullback, known as the "Haskell Hurricane."

It was a boiling hot day when Villanova's load of beef took the field with names like Urbellis, Di Filippo ... Corleone, Tattaglia, Luca Brazzi. The field was dry, baked brown, and the visitors developed a habit of coughing and spitting as dust came up a foot off the ground — and hung there — every time John Kimbrough fell on it, after trampling Wildcats. The result was a surprising 33-to-7 victory for Texas A&M, a score that raised eyebrows throughout the East and didn't hurt the Aggies in the polls later on.

A&M endured only one close call during the regular season. That was the bizarre 6-to-2 victory over SMU in the rain and mud of Kyle Field at College Station. The Ags blamed the close score on the weather. The Mustangs, who were building toward an excellent team, blamed their loss on a fumble, and said wait till next year.

The Aggies didn't face another tough opponent until they reached the Sugar Bowl. There they met Tulane, the Southeastern Conference champion, which came in with an 8-0-1 record and a slippery all-crawfish halfback in Bobby Kellogg.

Kellogg and the Green Wave gave the Aggies a scare and even led by 13 to 7 with the final period half over. Fortunately, A&M's all-conference end, Herbie Smith, the smallest guy on the field, raced in and blocked Tulane's extra-point try after their go-ahead touchdown, and his effort turned out to be no small thing.

Kimbrough, who would plow through Tulane for 152 yards on the day, took over and scored after a long, desperate drive. The touchdown came on a play covering 18 yards and was typical of the Aggies' style.

Cotton Price, who played most of the game at quarterback for the ailing Marion Pugh, flipped a pass out in the flat to Herbie Smith, who lateraled the ball to Kimbrough, and the Haskell Hurricane took it home. Price then kicked the winning point. Final score: Aggies 14, Tulane 13.

The Aggies' John Kimbrough plows through TCU in 1939 game.

It may be of interest to compare the Aggies' record in '39 with the unbeaten teams they outpolled.

TEXAS A&M, No. 1			TENNESSEE, No. 2		
32	Oklahoma A&M	0	13	NC State	0
14	Centenary	0	40	Sewanee	0
7	Santa Clara	3	28	Chattanooga	0
33	Villanova	7	21	Alabama	0
20	TCU	6	17	Mercer	0
20	Baylor	0	20	LSU	0
27	Arkansas	0	34	The Citadel	0
6	SMU	2	13	Vanderbilt	0
19	Rice	0	19	Kentucky	0
20	Texas	0	7	Auburn	0

CORNELL, No. 3			SOUTHERN CALIFORNIA, No. 4		
19	Syracuse	6	7	Oregon	7 (tie)
20	Princeton	7	27	Washington State	0
47	Penn State	0	26	Illinois	0
23	Ohio State	14	26	California	0
13	Columbia	7	19	Oregon State	7
14	Colgate	12	33	Stanford	0
35	Dartmouth	6	20	Notre Dame	12
26	Penn	0	9	Washington	7
			0	UCLA	0 (tie)

The Aggies went into the next season, 1940, with virtually the same team, not to mention high hopes and swoll up expectations.

They'd lost only two starters — Joe Boyd and Herbie Smith — but John Kimbrough and the entire backfield returned, and the replacements for Boyd and Smith were two highly regarded cadets named Chip Routt and Bill (Jitterbug) Henderson.

Routt came with good bloodlines. He was the younger brother of Joe Routt, A&M's reckless All-America guard of 1936 and '37, a guy who played the game with no regard for his own life or limb. His teammates predicted he would soldier the same way, and he did. In 1944, seven years later, Capt. Joe Routt, now of the United States Infantry, was awarded the Bronze Star posthumously after getting himself killed by charging a fortified German position at the Battle of the Bulge.

As for Jitterbug Henderson, a lad from Houston, he might as well have been a hero out of adventure comics. Before he was done, Henderson would earn 11 varsity letters in five different sports — football, basketball, baseball, track, and swimming. Along with all that, he would become the campus heavyweight boxing champion, the handball champion, three years all-conference in basketball, an All-American javelin thrower, and a 1941 All-America end in football.

With Kimbrough thundering to another All-America season along with Guard Marshall Robnett, and with four other Aggies having all-conference seasons, there was only one team on the 1940 schedule that could possibly stand in the way of

A&M and the Rose Bowl. That was SMU — and this was clearly the best Mustang eleven since '35.

Texas A&M went into that game with a 6-0 record, having beaten Texas A&I, Tulsa, UCLA, TCU, Baylor, and Arkansas. SMU was 4-0-1 with wins over UCLA, North Texas State, Auburn, Texas, and a tie with Pitt.

Hence, a Poll Bowl.

It was played in SMU's Ownby Stadium on November 9, which was a fortunate date in my case. The Frogs were off that week. I had no obligation to be in TCU Stadium rooting for the homefolks. I was free to catch the all-important A&M-SMU game on the radio at 2:30 in the afternoon, Kern Tips calling the action, but only after I caught Bill Stern calling the all-important Michigan-Minnesota game on the radio earlier.

I was well aware that undefeated and untied Michigan going up against undefeated and untied Minnesota — Tom Harmon vs. Bruce Smith — was the same thing as 1940's "Game of the Century."

Kimbrough rambles through the mud and Mustangs in 1940 showdown.

1940 Teaxas A&M-SMU game

SMU quarterback Ray Mallouf

SMU fullback Presto Johnston

If you think I sat staring at the radio for five hours that day wishing there was a picture in it, you're right. Unlike today. Today there *is* a picture in the radio, but I only stare at it if there's a college football game, a rerun of "The Larry Sanders Show," or an impeachment trial to watch.

I'd liked to have watched both John Kimbrough and Old 98, Tom Harmon, that day. I'd seen Kimbrough knock down Frogs when the '39 Aggies came to Fort Worth. Jarrin' John at 6-3, 222. He often ran straight up, carrying the ball like an apple in one hand, but tacklers seemed to, like, bounce off his hips. And when he'd get up steam, he could blast his way through whole piles of human debris.

Tom Harmon I'd only seen in newsreels, when the Worth or Hollywood theater downtown would show the weekly football highlights before Bette Davis or Barbara Stanwyck came on to smoke cigarettes and kill their husbands. Old 98 was the niftiest broken-field runner I'd ever seen and wore the greatest helmet ever designed, and I hated to hear him slipping down in the rain and mud so many times that day near the Minnesota end zone. I listened in utter frustration as Michigan frittered away so many scoring chances that Minnesota won the "Game of the Century," and with it the eventual national championship, by the score of 7 to 6.

Ironically, although they were hundreds of miles and rivers and hills apart, it rained a log floater that Saturday at both the Michigan-Minnesota game in Minneapolis and the A&M-SMU game in Dallas.

Thus, for the Aggies and Mustangs it was another showdown in what's known to sportswriters as your "sea of mud."

The lineups for that soggy, slippery Poll Bowl in Dallas:

TEXAS A&M		SMU
Jim Sterling	LE	Kelly Simpson
Ernie Pannell	LT	Joe Pasqua
Marshall Robnett	LG	Jake Fawcett
Tommy Vaughn	C	Raymond Pope
Chuck Henke	RG	Ted Ramsey
Chip Routt	RT	Lynn Bostick
Bill Henderson	RE	Roland Goss
Marion Pugh	Q	Ray Mallouf
Derace Moser	LH	Johnnie Clement
Jimmy Thomason	RH	Will Mullenweg
John Kimbrough	FB	Presto Johnston

Those Mustangs, incidentally, were very good. They would become known as "the Forgotten Champions," for they wound up sharing the conference title with A&M. Why and how comes later. Right now, here's how the most celebrated writer in the Ownby press box saw the affair:

By HENRY McLEMORE

United Press Staff Correspondent

DALLAS, Tex., Nov. 9 — Led by that pigskin pulverizer from the Plains, Jarrin' John Kimbrough, the Texas Aggies rolled through the rain and mud to their 18th consecutive victory today with a 19 to 7 triumph over their hottest rivals, the S.M.U. Mustangs.

A sellout crowd of more than 27,000 saw Kimbrough finally break loose from the corral the Mustangs had built around him, and single-handedly pound and maul and bruise his way for the touchdown that broke a 7-7 tie and the Mustangs' hearts.

Big John, his 222 pounds increased to 240 by equipment and mud, bore into the S.M.U. line seven times on this payoff drive, gaining 31 of the 35 yards needed. There wasn't any deceit in John's running. The Mustangs knew he was coming and where he was going to hit. They just couldn't stop him.

The S.M.U. linesmen charged viciously, met Kimbrough at the scrimmage line, and he would stage a one-man battle with them. He always won. First the line would bend under the impact of his rush, and then it would break as he churned his great legs and bulled his head and shoulders.

When Kimbrough finally crossed the goal to make the score 13 to 7, the ball game was over, although the brilliant Ray Mallouf's passing with a slippery ball was always a threat for S.M.U. Mallouf's 33-yard toss had produced the tying score, and sent Mustang fans into a wild celebration. They had lost a close contest 6 to 2 in the mud a year ago and had thirsted 12 months for this rematch.

The final Aggie touchdown came on a blocked punt near the end of the final period, but it was anticlimactic. The customers had come to see the mighty Kimbrough in action and he had delivered.

Today's game filled every stadium seat and the crush was so great in the temporary bleachers behind the south goal that they collapsed in the first quarter, throwing 600 fans to the ground.

After the Aggies plundered Rice 25 to 0 the following week, a game in which Jitterbug Henderson caught three touchdown passes, maybe you couldn't blame them for feeling a little cocky.

They held the nation's longest win streak at 19. They had become the first school in Southwest Conference history to repeat as champions. They were 8-0 for the season and No. 1 in the polls. John Kimbrough and Marshall Robnett had been named to countless All-America teams. The Rose Bowl had already said it wanted them. And they were three-touchdown favorites in their last game of the regular season, the one in Austin on November 28, Thanksgiving Day, against a University of Texas team that had yet to find itself and had already been soundly beaten by Rice and SMU. The Texas Aggies had several good reasons to think their Rose Bowl train couldn't be stopped by anything but an act of God — and God was obviously an Aggie.

TEXAS A&M 1939 NATIONAL CHAMPIONS

Halfback
Jimmy
Thomason

All-America fullback John
Kimbrough

End
Herbie Smith

All-America
tackle
Joe Boyd

Guard
Chuck Henke

Halfback
Derace Moser
Inset: Bill
Conatser

Quarterback Marion Pugh
Inset: Cotton Price

Center Tommy Vaughn

All-America guard
Marshall Robnett

Tackle Ernie Pannell

End Jim Sterling

NINE

EVERY HEADLINE writer on every paper in Texas had the same idea, and the black banners across the state on November 29, 1940, all said more or less the same thing. Something on the order of ...

LONGHORNS DERAIL ROSE BOWL EXPRESS!

Frankly, I never understood why Texas' 7-to-0 upset over the Aggies pleased so many people, even Longhorn fans.

Why wouldn't it have been a better deal for a Southwest Conference team to get to go to the Rose Bowl? Like, you know, it didn't exactly happen every day.

Strange, inexplicable upsets never fascinated me all that much, anyhow. As a kid I wanted the New York Yankees and Joe DiMaggio to win every World Series, Joe Louis to win every fight, Whirlaway to win every horse race, and Ben Hogan or Byron Nelson to win every golf tournament.

The world made more sense when favorites won stuff. What, I was supposed to find it charming if the Japs won World War II?

Years later, when Darrell Royal was the coach at the University of Texas, he said it best about upset teams.

"They're like cockroaches," he said. "All they do is crawl around and mess things up."

The Longhorns of Coach Dana X. Bible in 1940 weren't cockroaches by any means. They were all highly recruited athletes, and when you consider how good they were a year later, in 1941, the derailing of Texas A&M's Rose Bowl Express becomes somewhat less of an upset.

On that Thanksgiving Day the Longhorns scored in four plays in the first 58 seconds after receiving the kickoff. Pete Layden ran a sweep to the right on the first play, suddenly stopped, looked, and floated a pass back to Jack Crain, who had drifted out to the left sideline. A 30-yard gain to A&M's 35-yard line. A Layden pass down the middle fell incomplete. Then Layden ran a sweep to the left, but stopped again and hurled a 34-yard pass over Kimbrough's head to his wingback, Noble Doss, who was flying down the right sideline. Doss made a remarkable circus catch — a blind, Willie Mays, over-his-head type of thing — and tumbled out of bounds on the Aggies' one-yard line. Pete Layden promptly plunged over for the touchdown, and Jack Crain kicked the point.

Most people listening on the radio didn't think much about Texas grabbing a 7-0 lead. Most people were stuffed with turkey and dressing, sprawled on grandmama's carpet, trying to keep awake so they could hear Jarrin' John Kimbrough score three or four touchdowns.

The Aggies marched up and down the field for the next 59 minutes and two seconds, frequently driving deep into Texas territory, occasionally inside the Longhorns' 10-yard line, but they couldn't buy a score.

"Cowboy Jack" Crain, "the Nocona Nugget," one of Texas' greatest running backs.

Texas' Noble Doss makes the impossible catch of Pete Layden's pass . . .

There were numerous reasons, as it turned out. Five of them were Texas interceptions. Noble Doss himself picked off three. Kimbrough gained more than 100 yards rushing, usually out of the spread-end formation, but each time the Ags drew close to the Texas end zone they'd try to surprise the Steers with passes, and it never worked.

The passes never fooled the "Immortal Thirteen," as they came to be known — the only 13 Texas players who took the field that day.

It shouldn't have mattered that A&M's regular quarterback, Marion Pugh, was hardly in the game at all. This was the nearest thing Norton's team could call on for an excuse. Pugh was suffering from an infected boil on his leg. But Pugh's replacement, the talented senior Marland Jeffrey, was, after all, the guy who kept piloting the Aggies up and down the field.

A&M's defeat allowed SMU to become co-champions of the conference. The Mustangs' fine season record of 8-1-1 put them securely among the nation's top 10 teams in the rankings, but even so, they were ignored by all the bowl committees and have been known as the "Forgotten Champions" ever since.

SMU's own city of Dallas chose the Aggies to host the Cotton Bowl after the Rose Bowl invited Nebraska. The Sugar Bowl preferred Tennessee and Boston

College over the Ponies, and the Orange Bowl chose Georgetown and Mississippi State over SMU.

Kimbrough and the other fabulous Aggie seniors closed out their careers by beating a tough Fordham team in the Cotton Bowl, 13 to 12, but the sting of the Texas upset would last a lifetime.

Kimbrough was more philosophical about it than most of his teammates. Reflecting on the upset a few years later, he said, "That was a real funny game. I think if we played 'em 900 times, we'd win 899 of 'em, but we couldn't beat 'em that day. They were really keyed up for us, and played a great game. I don't think anything could have helped us that day, not even a healthy Marion Pugh."

Coach Homer Norton may well have come closer to the truth of what happened right after the loss when he spoke to his weeping squad in the dressing room, the Rose Bowl dream shattered.

Norton said to the team, "This is perhaps the bitterest pill you will ever have to swallow, but there's one thing about it. If you can take what happened to you today as a lesson when you go out into life and don't get cocky and overconfident at some other important time, then this defeat might not be as bad as it seems."

Cocky and overconfident. His key words.

Then Norton himself retreated into a corner and wept.

Lot of lessons to be learned in football, of course. And most of those same tri-

. . . then Layden (11) bulls over for the touchdown.

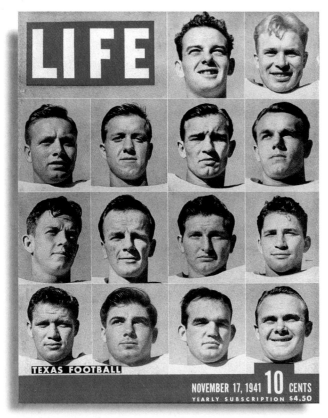

"The *Life* magazine 14": Left to right, the Texas Longhorns of 1941 are (top row) Wally Scott, end; Vernon Martin, blocking back; (second row) Spec Sanders, reserve halfback; Mal Kutner, end; Julian Garrett, tackle; Henry Harkins, center; (third row) Noble Doss, halfback; R.L. Harkins, reserve tailback; Preston Flanagan, end; Chal Daniel, guard; (bottom row) Buddy Jungmichel, guard; Pete Layden, tailback; Bo Cohenour, tackle; Jack Crain, halfback.

umphant Longhorns would learn a couple themselves, but not until they were on the cover of Life magazine in 1941.

This was the payoff of Dana X. Bible's five-year plan to bring fame and fortune back to University of Texas football. Texas' vigorous recruiting efforts had brought to Austin the most-wanted athletes in the state. They were now stacked two-deep and at some positions three-deep.

Jack Crain, the swift halfback, Pete Layden, the triple-threat fullback, Mal Kutner, the pass-catching end, and Chal Daniel, the all-around guard, were in the process of making All-America teams in '41, and five of the reserves — end Joe Parker, tackle Stan Mauldin, guard Harold Fischer, center Jack Sachse, and fullback Roy Dale McKay — would also be named to All-America teams by the end of 1943.

And this says nothing about all the other Longhorn notables, such as wingback Noble Doss, blocking back Vern Martin, reserve fullback R.L. Harkins, guards Buddy Jungmichel and Jack Freeman, tackles Julian Garrett, Bo Cohenour, and Zuehl Conoly, ends galore in Preston Flanagan, Wally Scott, Mike Sweeney, and Joe Schwarting, and a couple of fabled subs who could evade tacklers with skill — Spec Sanders and Max Minor.

It was their first six games that landed the Steers on the Life cover and moved them up to No. 1 in the polls, and had Southwest Conference football fans talking about the Rose Bowl again.

With first Crain and then Layden performing wonderous deeds, and the subs performing even more, the Longhorns rolled over Colorado 34 to 6, LSU 34 to 0, Oklahoma 40 to 7, Arkansas 48 to 14, Rice 46 to 0, and SMU 34 to 0. Crain, "the Nocona Nugget," was averaging 7.4 yards a carry, and Layden was throwing a touchdown pass every other time he touched the ball.

SMU Coach Matty Bell did his part in setting up the Longhorns for a fall. He said, "This is the greatest team in Southwest Conference history. Yeah, even better than my Rose Bowl team in '35. Why, I didn't have but 16 men. D.X. has three full teams!"

It's still a mystery how a lowlife Baylor club that would win only three games all season could tie these Longhorns 7 to 7 in Waco on November 8.

Four Longhorn regulars were out with injuries, it's true, and some others were only half-speed because of ailments, but so what? They had all that depth. What Texas was really fighting was "one of those days." It actually looked as if they'd scrape by. Even though they flubbed three scoring opportunities down close, they still held a 7-0 lead with only four minutes to play, with Baylor back on its own 18-yard line and a substitute, Kit Kittrell, in the lineup at tailback for the Bears' injured star, Jack Wilson. What chance did Baylor have at that point?

Most people said none.

Most people were still saying none as Kittrell's passes and scrambling runs kept a Bear drive going. Eventually Baylor found itself on Texas' 19-yard line with only 18 seconds left on the clock.

Still no chance, right? Except it was here that Kittrell took the snap, faded back, dodged this way and that, fooled around long enough to eat a box lunch, as Kern Tips might have said, and finally hurled a desperate pass into the end zone, which was where a Baylor guy named Bill Coleman, already down on his knees, caught the ball for a touchdown. Jack Wilson then limped onto the field and kicked the extra point that tied the nation's No. 1 team.

Foreheads were smote on both sides of the field.

The whole next week in Austin every Longhorn player and every Longhorn fan acted like a dear relative had passed on. Instead of the Texas players preparing for an excellent TCU team coming to town on Saturday, they mourned.

As Bible remembered it years later, "Everywhere you went that week there was gloom and lamenting, all of us sympathizing with each other. We'd been knocked down, but we shouldn't have stayed down. We should have gotten right back up and gotten ready for TCU. I take the blame for that. I can still get mad at myself for letting it happen."

The Longhorns looked like themselves again when they seized a 7-0 lead early in the TCU game, scoring on a double-lateral thing — Layden to Crain and back to Layden — that covered 36 yards.

But then Texas went into another lull, and TCU tied the game 7-7 late in the second quarter. The Frogs were without their star quarterback, Kyle Gillespie, a triple-threat operator who was as gifted as Sam Baugh and Davey O'Brien ever were — when he wasn't hurt. With Gillespie healthy from '39 through '41, the Frogs usually won the game. But Gillespie suffered leg injuries for three whole seasons. It was as if a higher authority had ruled that TCU didn't deserve another Baugh or O'Brien right away. And now against Texas Gillespie was recovering from a broken leg in the A&M game earlier in the season and was only available to punt.

One of Gillespie's replacements was Dean Bagley, a little tailback from San Saba. Bagley scored the Purple touchdown on an improvised journey after he was unable to find a pass receiver. He meandered 55 yards, side-stepping almost every player on the Texas team. It's estimated that

Bagley probably ducked and dodged his way 80 yards, total, on that run.

Thereafter, the Longhorns spent the day fouling up their own scoring chances again, as they had against Baylor. They recovered a fumble on the TCU 10-yard line and did nothing with it. They drove inside the Frogs' 10 once more and threw an interception. And yet another time, Mal Kutner, the All-America end, all alone near the TCU goal, dropped a 35-yard pass from Pete Layden.

This left TCU with nothing to do in the last two minutes but win the game. Into the Frog lineup came another backup for Kyle Gillespie. He was a sophomore, Emery Nix, but no ordinary soph. He was a much-wanted recruit with a strong throwing arm, a quarterback who'd led Corpus Christi to the state high school championship in 1938, a season in which he'd earned the nickname "Ice Water."

All Nix did was drive TCU 72 yards to the winning touchdown. He started it off with a 34-yard run of his own, and finished it by firing a 19-yard bullet into the end zone to another sophomore, halfback Van Hall, who was wide open and caught the pass in his stomach as the clock showed only 8 seconds left. TCU 14, Texas 7.

So put that on the the cover of *Life*, Frog fans suggested.

After that, the Longhorns had 12 days to get ready for Texas A&M on Thanksgiving, and maybe a long rest was what they needed. The Aggies still had Derace Moser and Jim Sterling left over from the national championship team of '39, but otherwise they were all new. Not that it mattered. They were 9-0, conference champions again, and No. 2 in the AP poll when they ran into a bunch of Longhorns who were eager to atone for their sins. Jack Crain rushed for 115 yards, Layden pitched a long touchdown pass to Kutner, and Texas humiliated A&M by 23 to 0.

That renewed the Longhorns' hopes for the Rose Bowl bid, and they were led to believe they still had the inside track, despite the loss and tie, but the invitation finally went to Duke instead. While they were waiting on the Pasadena decision, the Longhorns were forced to turn down the Sugar Bowl. Then when they missed out on the Rose Bowl, they were so angry about it they rejected a bid to the Orange Bowl. Miami promptly invited TCU. The Frogs accepted and on New Year's Day played a wild one with Georgia in which the Bulldogs' Frankie Sinkwich and TCU's Kyle Gillespie put on a show. Georgia held off a furious Purple comeback to win, 40 to 26. What the Longhorns did before that, however, was vent their anger on the field.

It was a decent Oregon team that came to Austin for the last game, a team that had barely lost a 12-7 game to Oregon State, the Pacific Coast's Rose Bowl representative. But everybody in orange jumped on poor old Oregon. When they got through Texas had won by 71 to 7, no typo.

Texas' season record in '41 was 8-1-1, but the Longhorns had come within 18 seconds against Baylor and 8 seconds against TCU of being undefeated, and in a low-scoring era of college football they'd averaged 40.4 points a game against their other eight opponents.

Such things were obviously considered by the syndicated Williamson Rankings. Williamson pronounced Texas the national champion in its final tabulations, rating the Longhorns over three undefeated teams.

You may now ponder the Longhorns' record in '41 compared with those of their distinguished rivals for No. 1:

TEXAS, No. 1

34	Colorado	6
34	LSU	0
40	Oklahoma	7
48	Arkansas	14
40	Rice	0
34	SMU	0
7	Baylor	7
7	TCU	14
23	Texas A&M	0
71	Oregon	7

MINNESOTA, No. 2

14	Washington	6
34	Illinois	6
39	Pittsburgh	0
7	Michigan	0
8	Northwestern	7
9	Nebraska	0
34	Iowa	13
41	Wisconsin	6

DUKE, No. 3

43	Wake Forest	14
19	Tennessee	0
50	Maryland	0
27	Colgate	14
27	Pittsburgh	7
14	Georgia Tech	0
56	Davidson	0
20	North Carolina	0
55	NC State	6

NOTRE DAME, No. 4

38	Arizona	7
19	Indiana	6
20	Georgia Tech	0
16	Carnegie Tech	0
49	Illinois	14
0	Army	0 (tie)
20	Navy	13
7	Northwestern	6
20	USC	18

The season ended with ironies scattered all over the place, like Jack Crain's footwork. It so happened that Texas' beating up of Oregon took place on Saturday, December 6, 1941 — and unless you're some kind of slug born to boomers, you know what occurred on Sunday, December 7, 1941.

TEXAS' 1941 NATIONAL CHAMPIONS

All-America end Mal Kutner

All-America halfback Jack Crain

Tackle Julian Garrett

Halfback Noble Doss

**Halfback
Spec Sanders**

End Preston Flanagan

All-America tailback Pete Layden

All-America guard Chal Daniel

Tackle Bo Cohenour

Guard Buddy Jungmichel

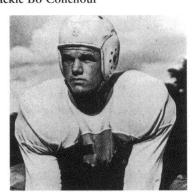

Center Henry Harkins

**Blocking back
Vernon Martin**

TEN

IMMEDIATELY after the Japs bombed Pearl Harbor — and we declared war on Hitler, Tojo, and Mussolini — a funny thing happend to Duke and Oregon State on their way to the Rose Bowl.

The Rose Bowl got moved to Durham, North Carolina.

Not the stadium in Pasadena, just the game.

And all because there was an instant blackout on the whole Pacific Coast. Fear went running around rampant and even plentiful that Yamamoto and his yellow-peril carriers were sitting only 100 yards off the beach of Santa Monica, their planes ready to bomb the Rose Bowl game, the Brown Derby, Schwab's Drugstore, and the back lot at Paramount.

There was also fear that if Yamamoto's planes weren't a threat, there was a saboteur among all the underpaid Beverly Hills gardners, and he'd be eager to blow up every rich, white Yankee dog in the Pasadena stadium.

But rather than see the game canceled, the good people of Durham went into a work, toil, and labor mode, and in just two weeks they enlarged the Duke University stadium from a capacity of 35,000 to 56,000, sold it out in three days, and said, "Right here's your Rose Bowl."

The game was then played on January 3, 1942, and the good people of Durham were rewarded by twice-beaten Oregon State, a 4-to-1 underdog, embarrassing their undefeated Blue Devils, 20 to 16.

The entire point is, if the Longhorns of 1941 had received the Rose Bowl invitation they anticipated — one their "inside source" had promised was on the way — the game would have been played in Austin, Texas!

Which would have meant no studio tours, no movie stars, no Musso & Frank, no gin and blondes. Would have been a tragedy.

But there'd be enough real tragedies. Too many.

This was the generation that went to war.

All these football teams that have been discussed on previous pages were part of it, and some of the grid stars weren't so lucky.

You've already heard about Joe Routt, Texas A&M's All-America guard of '36 and '37 who was killed at the Battle of the Bulge, but there were many other sacrifices.

Johnny Sprague, who quarterbacked SMU's national champions and Rose Bowl team in '35, who threw many a block for Bobby Wilson, was an officer in the

142nd Infantry. Shortly after the Salerno landing in a place called Altavilla, Italy, Sprague exposed himself to fire in an effort to locate a German gun emplacement and was killed. He was awarded the Silver Star posthumously.

Derace Moser and Herbie Smith, two starters on Texas A&M's national champions of '39, transferred their cadet commissions into the Army Air Corps. Moser, who was a sophomore wingback on the national champions and became an All-America tailback in '41, was killed in a crash in Florida in '42 during final flight training as a bomber pilot. Smith, an all-conference end in '39, was training to be a fighter pilot when he died in a crash landing in '42 near his air base in Pennsylvania.

Chal Daniel, Texas' All-America guard on the '41 national champions, was a lieutenant in the Army Air Corps in 1943 when he died in the crash of his basic trainer near New Braunfels, Texas.

Two of Daniel's Longhorn teammates died in combat. Mike Sweeney, one of Texas' top four ends in '41, went down in his bomber over Europe in 1944, and Red Goodwin, one of the "Immortal Thirteen" that upset A&M in '40, and would have been the starting center in '41 if he hadn't gone into the service, also went down in a bombing raid over Germany.

A half-dozen TCU letter-men paid the ultimate price, including Bob Balaban, an end, and Bill Ramsey, a halfback, two members of the '41 Orange Bowl squad. They died in bombing raids, Balaban over Germany, Ramsey over Rabaul.

COLLEGE FOOTBALL'S 10 BEST STADIUMS

(For atmosphere, and not necessarily in order)

• **ROSE BOWL**, Pasadena, California, 94,000.
(Not a bad seat in the house, unless UCLA loses.)

• **MICHIGAN STADIUM**, Ann Arbor, Michigan, 107,501.
(Impossible not to be in awe — or in love — with this place.)

• **TIGER STADIUM**, Baton Rouge, Louisiana, 80,000.
(Cozy and gives new meaning to the word loud when LSU is winning.)

• **NOTRE DAME STADIUM**, South Bend, Indiana, 80,012.
(The house that Rockne built. Enough said.)

• **STANFORD STADIUM**, Palo Alto, California, 85,500.
(One of the oldest of the biggest and still one of the best on campus.)

• **MICHIE STADIUM**, West Point, New York, 39,929.
(The cannons, the river, the Cadets. Best of the smallest. Total charm.)

• **MEMORIAL STADIUM**, Lincoln, Nebraska, 72,700.
(A Cornhusker relic, but from the top you see Wyoming.)

• **DARRELL ROYAL-TEXAS STADIUM**, Austin, Texas, 80,082. *(Heart of the campus, the track removed, capacity increased, and anything named for Darrell Royal ain't bad.)*

• **HUSKEY STADIUM**, Seattle, Washington, 72,500.
(Another tall old relic, but take a boat to the game.)

• **SANFORD STADIUM**, Athens, Georgia, 86,117.
(All leafy Georgia campus outside and the famous hedges inside.)

COLLEGE FOOTBALL'S 11 BEST ELEVENS

1. Southern Cal, 1972
Record: 12-0
Coach: John McKay
Star players: Anthony Davis, hb; Lynn Swan, wr; Charles Young, te; Mike Rae, qb; Sam (Bam) Cunningham, fb; Richard Wood, lb. *(Never had a close game. Mangled everybody, including Ohio State in the Rose Bowl.)*

2. Army, 1945
Record: 9-0
Coach: Red Blaik
Star players: Glenn Davis, hb; Doc Blanchard, fb; Arnold Tucker, qb; Hank Foldberg, e; DeWitt Counter, t; John Green, g. *(Yeah, it was a war year but Glenn went outside, Doc went inside, and they beat everybody 4,000 to 0.)*

3. Notre Dame, 1947
Record: 9-0
Coach: Frank Leahy
Star players: Johnny Lujack, qb; Terry Brennan, hb; Emil Sitko, hb; George Connor, t; Bill Fischer, g; Leon Hart, e.
(Most powerful, exciting, and glamorous of all Irish elevens.)

4. Texas, 1969
Record: 11-0
Coach: Darrell Royal
Star players: James Street, qb; Steve Worster, fb; Bob McKay, t; Cotton Speyrer, e; Jim Bertelsen, hb; Glen Halsell, lb.
(Pulverized nine straight, then showed the character to come from behind and win the school's two biggest games in history, against Arkansas and Notre Dame.)

5. Oklahoma, 1956
Record: 10-0
Coach: Bud Wilkinson
Star players: Tommy McDonald, hb; Jimmy Harris, qb; Clendon Thomas, hb; Billy Pricer, fb; Jerry Tubbs, c; Bill Krisher, g.
(This bunch didn't lose a game for three whole years, from '54 through '56, and pretty much stomped all their foes in the dirt.)

6. Alabama, 1934
Record: 10-0
Coach: Frank Thomas
Star players: Dixie Howell, hb; Don Hutson, e; Riley Smith, qb; Bill Lee, t; Charley Marr, g; "Little Joe" Riley, hb; Bear Bryant, e.
(Best and most dazzling of all the great 'Bama teams.)

7. Nebraska, 1971

Record: 13-0

Coach: Bob Devaney

Star players: Johnny Rodgers, hb; Jerry Tagge, qb; Jeff Kinney, hb; Rich Glover, mg; Larry Jacobson, t.

(Still the best Nebraska team, and the one that overcame Oklahoma in the Game of the Year, Decade, and Century.)

8. Ohio State, 1968

Record: 10-0

Coach: Woody Hayes

Star players: Rex Kern, qb; Jim Otis, fb; Dave Foley, t; Bruce Jankowski, e; Jack Tatum, db; Jim Stillwagon, mg.

(They were young, they were impulsive, they were fiery, and they did it all, including a Rose Bowl win over the great USC-O.J. team.)

9. Miami, 1987

Record: 12-0

Coach: Jimmy Johnson

Star players: Steve Walsh, qb; Michael Irvin, wr; Daniel Stubbs, lb; Bennie Blades, db; Mel Bratton, fb.

(*Talk about rising to the occasion. This is the gang that knocked off unbeaten Florida State for No. 1 in a thriller, then whipped unbeaten Oklahoma in another battle for No. 1 in the Orange Bowl.*)

10. TCU, 1938

Record: 11-0

Coach: Dutch Meyer

Star Players: Davey O'Brien, qb; Ki Aldrich, c; I.B. Hale, t; Don Looney, e; Earl Clark, hb; Johnny Hall, hb.

(*Overwhelming every opponent, seven of them on the road, O'Brien led the nation in total offense and passing, and the first-team defense allowed only two touchdowns all season.*)

11. Michigan, 1940

Record: 7-1

Coach: Fritz Crisler

Star players: Tom Harmon, hb; Forest Evashevski, qb; Bob Westfall, fb; Al Wistert, t; Ed Frutig, e.

(*With Harmon's broken-field running setting a new standard in that department, this was the best team that ever lost one game — and it took a rainy day, muddy field, and Minnesota's successful extra-point for it to happen.*)

Grassy Hinton was the Frogs' most conspicuous casualty. Hinton had been a starting halfback as a sophomore on TCU's first conference championship team of '29. A triple-threat gentleman, Hinton took over as quarterback on the '30 and '31 teams, leading those elevens to consecutive seasons of 9-2-1 in which they barely missed out on two more titles. Hinton was lost in '44 in a bombing raid in the East Indies.

Of all the Southwest Conference players who served in the Second World War, none was more courageous than Baylor's Jack Lummus, a starting end on the '39 and '40 teams. He became a lieutenant in the Marines and wound up on Iwo Jima in March of '45. Though twice wounded in the fighting, he single-handedly advanced and destroyed three fortified Japanese bunkers before he was killed by a land mine. Lummus is buried in the 5th Division cemetery on Iwo Jima. A year after he was killed in action, his mother in Ennis, Texas, received the Congressional Medal of Honor he was awarded for his act of extreme heroism.

A pause now to mention some of the other more prominent football heroes from around the country who gave their lives in WWII.

Ens. Nile Kinnick — Iowa's All-America tailback and Heisman winner of 1939. Killed in '43 in the Caribbean while trying to crash-land his disabled fighter plane.

Capt. Al Blozis — All-America tackle at Georgetown in 1940 and onetime world record holder in the shotput. Killed in action in '44 in the mountains of France.

Capt. Waddy Young — All-America end at Oklahoma in 1938. Went down with his B-29 in a bombing mission over Tokyo in 1945.

Lt. Clint Castleberry — Georgia Tech's All-America tailback in 1942. He led the Engineers to a 9-1 record and the Cotton Bowl as a freshman. He was killed in action in '44 when his plane went down in the Mediterranean.

Capt. Don Scott — All-America halfback and captain of Ohio State's conference champions in 1939. Killed in '43 when his malfunctioning bomber crashed in England.

Cpl. Tony Butkovich — A star at Illinois in '42 before the V-7 program transferred him to Purdue. There, he became an All-America fullback on Purdue's undefeated team of 1943. A fighting Marine, he was killed in action on Okinawa in 1945.

Lt. Dave Schreiner — An All-America end on Wisconsin's national champions of 1942. Schreiner was killed in action on Okinawa two months after his Wisconsin teammate, tackle Bob Baumann, and Tony Butkovich.

Maj. Bill (Memphis Bill) Mallory — All-America fullback on Yale's undefeated team of 1923. Perished in '45 in the crash of a transport plane over Europe.

Col. Paul Bunker — Army's first great football hero. An All-America at West Point at tackle in '01, at fullback in '02. An artillery officer who helped defend Corregidor in the Philippines, Bunker eventually died in '43 after having been brutalized for two years as a Japanese POW.

Lt. Jack Chevigny — A reliable halfback for Notre Dame in '28 and the guy who scored the winning touchdown over Army after Knute Rockne made his "Gipper" speech. Later the head coach for four years at the University of Texas. One of more than 6,000 U.S. Marines who were killed in action on Iwo Jima in '45.

Capt. Walter (Pop) Scholl — Star back on Cornell's unbeaten team of '39 and "fifth down" team of '40. Reported missing in action in '43 when his plane never returned from a mission in North Africa.

Capt. Bob Faurot — Younger brother of Missouri Coach Don Faurot and backfield mate of Paul Christman on Missouri's Orange Bowl team of '39. Decorated for bravery several times, Faurot died when his fighter plane was shot down in '43 during the Battle of the Bismarck Sea.

Lt. Young Bussey — A top halfback and passer on LSU's Sugar Bowl team of 1937. Bussey was killed in action while leading a landing party in the invasion of the Philippines in '44.

Sgt. Nick Basca — All-around backfield ace on Villanova's undefeated team of '38, and the Wildcats' standout in their intersectional loss to Texas A&M in '39. Who could have predicted that three players on the field that day in Tyler, Texas — the Aggies' Derace Moser and Herbie Smith, and Villanova's Nick Basca — would all die in the war? Basca was killed in action serving with Gen. George Patton's 3rd Army in France.

Capt. Butch Luther — Outstanding halfback and breakaway runner on Nebraska's Rose Bowl team of 1940. A little over two years later, in February of '43, Luther was killed in action by snipers at the Anzio beachhead.

Calling to attention the ultimate sacrifices of these few well-known players is not to ignore two other things. That hundreds of other athletes, from colleges large and small, also sacrificed their lives in that war, and that thousands of others served willingly and often with valor when they went off to fight for duty, honor, country.

It was that kind of deal. Hard for your boomers and yuppie self-indulgents to understand today, of course.

LEGENDARY LINEMEN OF THE SWC

Weldon Humble, Rice's All-America guard, 1946

A&M's 1936-37 All-America guard Joe Routt

TCU's All-America tackle Bob Lilly, 1960

Aggie All-America guard Marshall Robnett, 1940

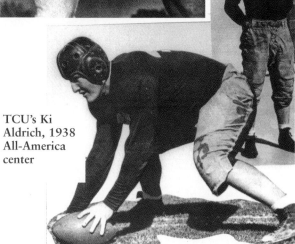

TCU's Ki Aldrich, 1938 All-America center

Barton (Bochey) Koch, All-America guard at Baylor, 1930

"The All-Conference Line": TCU's champions of 1932 overwhelmed opponents up front. Left to right, the All-SWC players were Pappy Pruitt, Foster Howell, Johnny Vaught, J.W. Townsend, Lon Evans, Ben Boswell, and Dan Salkeld, the other end.

ELEVEN

.J. LAMBERT said, "It don't seem right for a college football player to go off and get killed in a war. Young guy like that."

"Or anybody else," Billy Clyde said.

"Yeah, but a football player," T.J. frowned.

"Lot of soda jerks bought it, you watch your war movies," Tommy Earl contributed.

"Soda jerks?" said T.J. "You sayin' more soda jerks got killed in the war than football players?"

Tommy Earl: "Kids from Brooklyn ... Texas ... farms in Iowa. Fighting for our right to eat apple pie and boo the Dodgers."

T.J. said, "You makin' fun of them what got killed in the war, or is it you're just missin' a blade in your disposal?"

"I'm not joking about kids gettin' killed in the war," Tommy Earl said. "I'm talking about your World War Two movies. All I know is, ever time a soda jerk winds up in a foxhole and shows a buddy a Kodak picture of his sweetheart back home, you can bet your stack he's gonna get his ass shot off by a buck-tooth Jap or Hitler German."

It was chicken-and-dumplings night at He's Not Here, and we were having dinner at the round table in the back of the room.

The joint began serving dinner about a year ago, after Tommy Earl got another DWI. There was only one dish each night, and the regulars had taken a hand in the selections.

The lineup was butter beans and corn bread on Monday, cold meat loaf sandwich on light bread on Tuesday, fried-in-cornmeal catfish on Wednesday, homemade corned beef hash with truck-stop eggs on Thursday, chicken and slick dumplings on Friday, grease-down-your-wrist cheeseburgers on Saturday, and no-strangers chicken fried steak with cream gravy on Sunday.

He's Not Here didn't try to do barbecue and Tex-Mex. You couldn't go up against Railhead for barbecue and Mi Cocinita for Tex-Mex. Not unless you wanted to get your face slapped.

Tommy Earl was one of the owners and people had suggested to him that he ought to serve the chicken and slick dumplings on Wednesday and the catfish on Friday, to accommodate his Catholic customers.

"We don't cater to foreigners," he said.

The University of
Texas' "Sweet Bobby"
Layne, "the Blond
Bomber." Four years
All-Conference, he was
a consensus All-America
in 1947.

On the wall behind our table were enlarged and framed photos of some local celebrities, past and present. Billy Clyde, T.J., and Jim Tom Pinch were up there in an arrangement with Gov. W. Lee (Pappy) O'Daniel, Ginger Rogers, Ben Hogan, Rogers Hornsby, Tincy Eggleston and Gene Paul Norris.

Eggleston and Norris were two of Fort Worth's best-known underworld characters. They'd wound up wearing cement swimsuits.

Jim Tom, as you may know, was the sportswriter who'd made his name on the *Fort Worth Light & Shopper* and then moved to New York to play hurt for magazines. In the photo he was wearing his trademark khaki jacket that looked like it had come under heavy epaulet attack. The hint of a grin was on his face, and he'd signed the photo, which said:

"To my friends in He's Not Here — I can still smile even though Janet Cooke got my Pulitzer again."

That was supposed to be funny if you knew anything about journalism.

The network TV crew had come and gone. Five earnest young men, one mystified young woman. No Frankenburger.

One of the earnest young men wore a bright blue coat, a red tie, and an orange face. The mystified young woman wore a black pants suit with heels, short jagged blonde hair, and big green eyes. They were the announcers nobody had ever seen or heard of before.

The other earnest young men wore dirty jeans and faded Polo shirts. They were the cameraman, the sound man, the lighting man, and the producer. "We're just stockpiling," the producer said to Tami Kay.

The minidress worked her way over to the producer. "I'm told y'all want to use me for somethin'," she said.

"Oh?" said the producer. "Who told you that?"

"My girlfriend Tina. She said she did you at a golf tournament in Dallas last spring. Isn't your name Clark?"

"It certainly could be."

"Y'all from New York or Hollywood?"

"Connecticut."

"Where's that?" she squinted.

The producer led the minidress over to a wall behind the table where Wayne and Ralph were sitting. The tired salesmen were slumped in their chairs, longneck beer bottles all over their table.

The producer said to the minidress, "You stand here and look at the pictures on the wall while we interview these two gentlemen. You'll be very prominent in the background. Act interested in the wall."

The crew set up and the man with the orange face asked Wayne how big he thought this TCU-Southern Cal game was. While the minidress stared blankly at the wall and Ralph smoked, the mike was held out to Wayne.

Wayne said to the mike, "Dogass me. Cowshit I know? Asshole Ralph, he'll toilet to you."

Ralph giggled, flipped ashes on the floor, and said, "Dang, I hadn't heard that since the fifth grade at E.M. Daggett Elementary."

The minidress was still staring at the wall as the crew moved away to another table.

They probably made another mistake in asking this bureau for an interview, sitting me down in a chair facing the mystified young woman. She held a clipboard in her lap with questions on it.

She said, "I understand you saw Doc Walker play football when he was at SMU? Was he really as great as they say?"

"Doak," I said.

"Dazzling Doak" Walker, "the Mustang Miracle Man." A three-year consensus All-America tailback at SMU, 1947, 1948 and 1949, he was the most publicized player in college football history — and one of the most exciting.

LIFE

DOAK WALKER
OF
SOUTHERN
METHODIST

SEPTEMBER 27, 1948 20 CENTS
YEARLY SUBSCRIPTION $6.00

Doak Walker's leaping catch of a long pass was the play of the game.

"What?"

"It's Doak Walker, not Doc."

"Doak?"

"D-o-a-k. Doak."

She made a note, then said, "And, uh ... he wore a famous number. Seventy-seven, I believe."

"No. Doak Walker wore 37. Seventy-seven was Doc Grange."

"Ah-ha," she nodded, making another note.

"Still rolling," the cameraman said.

When she next asked what it was that made Doak Walker so special, it was easy for a geezer to hog the mike.

To start with, anybody with good sense who ever saw him play more than once would say he was the greatest college player who ever lived. That's right. Ever lived. Pound for pound, sinew for sinew, fiber for fiber.

Doak played both ways in an era of free substitution. He ran, passed, received, returned, punted, tackled, blocked, placekicked, and intercepted in the three seasons of 1947, 1948, and 1949 when he was a consensus All-America tailback.

At 5-10 and 165 pounds, Doak was a graceful, winning, do-everything athlete who looked even more streamlined in the new low-quarter shoes. He was the first player I ever saw wear low-quarters. He seemed to thrive on the suspense, the drama, of a close game. He was movie-star handsome, incredibly photogenic, which had something to do with him becoming the magazine-cover king — *Life*, *Look*, *Collier's*, etc. — easily the most publicized college player ever. For three full years, mind you. And yet his modesty never let all the acclaim move him. His

A great escape artist, Doak Walker makes a Longhorn miss.

teammates adored him, always looked to him for leadership, for one more miracle on the field, which he usually provided. Even his rivals admired and respected him.

Doak Walker was the ideal postwar hero.

The game that went a long way toward making Doak the ideal postwar hero was the first postwar Poll Bowl — another one I happened to see in person with my own eyes.

It was the SMU-Texas game in Dallas on November 1, 1947.

This was the hottest ticket since the TCU-SMU game of '35. The game was so huge, it had to be moved from the 26,000-seat Ownby Stadium on SMU's campus to the 45,000-seat Cotton Bowl at Dallas' State Fair Park. The Cotton Bowl had no upper deck at the time, but this was the game that eventually upper-decked it, turned it into "the house that Doak built," for Walker was only a sophomore in '47.

Many more home games to play.

The SMU-Texas game that day matched undefeated, united teams that were ranked No. 3 and No. 4 in the polls — Michigan and Notre Dame were duking it out over No. 1 and No. 2 at the time.

Their season records at the kickoff were explanation enough for why there was spilling-over standing-room only in the Cotton Bowl.

TEXAS (6-0)			SMU (5-0)		
33	Texas Tech	0	22	Santa Clara	6
38	Oregon	13	35	Missouri	19
34	North Carolina	0	21	Oklahoma A&M	14
34	Oklahoma	14	14	Rice	0
21	Arkansas	6	7	UCLA	0
12	Rice	0			

As important as anything else, if not more so, was the fact that the game featured the long-awaited duel between those two glamorous lads, Doak Walker and Bobby Layne. They were both headed for All-America acclaim but in a twist of fate that was quite unique, they were close pals. This dated back to their days as star players and teammates at Dallas' Highland Park High.

Doak and Bobby would become teammates again in the early 1950s, leading the Detroit Lions to two NFL championships, but on that gray, blustery afternoon in the Cotton Bowl they were deadly rivals.

Aside from Walker and Layne's friendship and their unbeaten records, the two teams had nothing else in common. Texas under its new coach, Blair Cherry, now ran the T-formation and was loaded with talent. SMU got by with 60-minute men in a platoon era, and a generous portion of sleight-of-hand. While Matty Bell was still the head coach, the Ponies ran out of Assistant Coach Rusty Russell's "Y" formation, Doak at tailback taking a direct snap from center and then doing all sorts of mysterious things with it. Spins, laterals, passes, reverses, and a favorite gimmick, the "flicker play." This was an often successful bit of trickery whereby Walker would take off in one direction, then sneakily put the ball on his hip, a teammate would seemingly come out of nowhere, take the ball off the hip, and set sail in the opposite direction, fervently hoping he'd fooled an entire continent.

Walker scampers in the "Game of the Decade."

The lineups for the game that upper-decked the house that Doak built:

S.M.U.		TEXAS
Dick Reinking	LE	Max Bumgardner
Joe Ethridge	LT	Dick Harris
Brownie Lewis	LG	Joe Magliolo
Cecil Sutphin	C	Joel Williams
Earl Cook	RG	Errol Fry
John Hamburger	RT	Ed Kelley
Sid Halliday	RE	Dale Schwartzkopf
Gil Johnson	Q	Bobby Layne
Doak Walker	LH	Byron Gillory
Paul Page	RH	Jimmy Canady
Dick McKissack	F	Tom Landry

You read it right. That's the same Tom Landry in the Longhorns' backfield who later in life was the only coach the Dallas Cowboys ever had — until Jimmy Johnson, Barry Switzer, and what's his name.

The Longhorns were so deep in talent, their subs practically read like a Texas High School Hall of Fame. In the line: Peppy Blount, George Petrovich, Charley Tatom, Vic Vasicek, Danny Wolfe, Jack Halfpenny, Dick Rowan. In the backfield:

Billy Pyle, Randall Clay, Bubba Shands, Ray Borneman, Perry Samuels, Raymond Jones, Bobby Coy Lee, Frank Guess, Travis Raven, Paul Campbell, Allen Lawler.

Maybe if they'd all been on the field at once they could have handled Doak that afternoon, but I'll let an old cigar-chewing veteran of deadline wars tell it. He had to write the fastest story.

By HAROLD V. RATLIFF

Associated Press Sports Writer

DALLAS, Nov. 1 — Magnificent Doak Walker passed, ran, and kicked Southern Methodist to a 14-13 victory over Texas today in a thrilling offensive duel that left the Mustangs the only undefeated, untied team in the great Southwest.

The little miracle man from Dallas bested Bobby Layne, his schoolboy pal of yesterday, in the heralded individual battle of stars. But even in defeat, Layne, Texas' "blond bomber," was a glittering standout in a clash that had an overflow crowd of 46,000 in a continuous uproar.

A Walker pass set up the first SMU touchdown and he leaped to make an amazing catch of a long pass from Gil Johnson that led to the other. After both touchdowns Walker planted the extra points through the goal posts, and this made the big difference in the end.

The great pony backfield of 1948 and 1949: Doak Walker, Paul Page, Dick McKissack and Kyle Rote.

The Methodists broke in front three minutes after the game started. Paul Page romped 81 yards on the opening kickoff, racing all the way to Texas' 19-yard line after taking a surprise handoff from Frank Payne. Walker quickly passed 15 yards to fullback Dick McKissack on the four. McKissack made a yard at center. Then Walker pulled the old "flicker play," another bit of Mustang magic. He rammed into the Texas line but put the ball on his hip. Paul Page, coming from his wingback position, took the ball from Walker and fled around his left end to score standing up.

Layne roared back to tie the score in the second quarter.

After Byron Gillory ran a punt back to the SMU 32, Layne pitched to Dale Schwartzkopf for eight and to Max Bumgardner for a first down at the SMU 13. Tom Landry and Jimmy Canady took turns hammering the SMU line until Landry bucked over from the one. Frank Guess came on to kick the extra point.

It wasn't tied for long. Southern Methodist grabbed the lead back before the half ended. The big play in the drive was a 54-yard pass from Gil Johnson to Doak Walker. It came on one of those formations where the Mustangs insert the passer, Johnson, into the lineup for the blocking back, Howard Parker or Bob Ramsey.

Johnson let fly with a heave that Walker soared into the air and brought down on his fingertips at about the Texas 30. He angled in a dash for the goal. Byron Gillory caught up and nudged him out of bounds at the one, but to no avail. McKissack scored on the next play.

Layne's passing barrage in a 72-yard drive got the other Texas score early in the fourth quarter. He hit Schwartzkopf for 21 and Blount for 26 and then Gillory for 14 and the touchdown. But this time, Frank Guess's try for point was wobbly and wide.

The game more than lived up to its expectations. It was a furious conflict for two hours, and when it was over Doak Walker had overshadowed every player on the field to give SMU the winning edge.

The more devout fans of Doak, which includes your typist, like to argue that he should have been the first — and perhaps the only — two-time winner of the Heisman.

He won it in '48, of course, and was third in the voting in '47 and '49. What Doakees and Doakors argue is that '47 was his best season. He just didn't have the lore strength of Johnny Lujack or Bob Chappuis, which is to say SMU didn't have the lore strength of Notre Dame or Michigan.

Doak did win the Maxwell award in '47, which showed that at least a certain group of people weren't swayed by South Bend or Ann Arbor.

Little known fact: in leading SMU to a 9-0-1 season in '47, Doak averaged 57 minutes a game, going both ways in that era of platoon ball. Week by week, here's all he did:

★ Ran 97 and 44 yards for touchdowns in the 22-to-6 win over Santa Clara in San Francisco.

★ Ran 76 and 57 yards for touchdowns in the 35-to-19 victory over Missouri.

★ Had a 30-yard run, ran three yards for one touchdown, passed 15 yards for another touchdown, and placekicked all three extra points in the 21-to-14 win over Oklahoma A&M.

★ Had a 35-yard run, plunged one yard for a touchdown and kicked both extra points in the 14-to-0 win over Rice.

★ Ran three yards for the touchdown and kicked the extra point in the 7-to-0 win over UCLA in Los Angeles.

★ Caught a 54-yard pass that set up a touchdown and kicked the winning extra points that beat Texas 14 to 13 in the "Game of the Year."

★ Played brilliant defense and combined with Gil Johnson to complete 16 of 18 passes in the aerial assault that beat Texas A&M 13 to 0.

★ Intercepted two passes, ran 17 yards to set up his two-yard touchdown run, and kicked both points in the 14-to-6 win over Arkansas.

★ Had dazzling runs of 76, 65 and 59 yards in his "greatest game" as he kept bringing the Mustangs back from certain defeat to gain a last-minute 19-to-19 tie with TCU.

While Lujack and Chappuis were great players, to be sure, nothing they did that season came close to matching Doak's exploits.

It should also be stated that SMU's schedule in '47 was far stronger than Notre Dame's or Michigan's, not that it counted for anything.

Seven of SMU's 10 opponents played .500 ball or better, mostly better, and won a total of 52 games. Chappuis and Michigan met teams that won only 34 games. Lujack and the Irish went up against nine teams that won only 29 games.

The lesson to be learned in all this was simple. Don't jack around with lore. Jack with lore, you get your ass kicked.

THE SIX HEISMAN WINNERS OF THE SWC

John David Crow, A&M, 1957

Doak Walker, SMU, 1948

Davey
O'Brien,
TCU, 1938

Earl Campbell, Texas, 1977

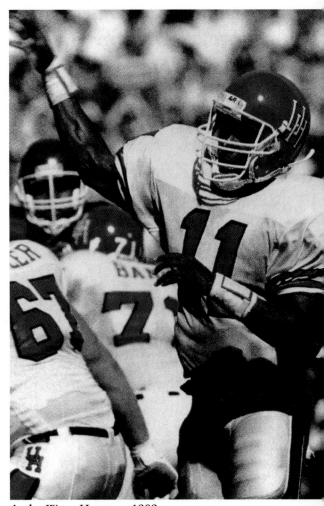

Andre Ware, Houston, 1989

Ricky Williams, Texas, 1998

TWELVE

TOMMY EARL wanted to know if I was serious when I said Doak Walker should have been a two-time Heisman winner.

"You didn't see him play," I said.

Tommy Earl said that was true, he didn't, seeing as how he'd probably been in the process of being conceived about that time. Most likely before his mama and daddy had gotten married, and were rolling around in the back seat of Frecklebelly Kennerdine's Plymouth with the windows fogged up.

T.J. said he couldn't imagine who might have conceived him — his mama and daddy never could stand to look at each other.

Billy Clyde said he was pretty sure he'd been born in a manger.

Wrestling the topic back to pigskin gladiators, I said I'd seen every single Heisman winner play football, either live or on film or on television, and what's more, I'd known about 25 of them personally, and therefore I knew a good deal more about it than most of the talk-show, drive-time loudmouths who voted on the thing these days.

Matter of fact, revising history is one of the more amusing things you can do in a bar. So we played the Heisman game for a while. You name the winner and the year and I either agree or name the guy who might have been more deserving. It came out like this:

WHO WON	WHO SHOULD HAVE
1935 Jay Berwanger, Chicago	Bobby Wilson, SMU
1936 Larry Kelley, Yale	Sam Baugh, TCU
1937 Clint Frank, Yale	Marshall Goldberg, Pitt
1938 Davey O'Brien, TCU	**Davey O'Brien, TCU**
1939 Nile Kinnick, Iowa	John Kimbrough, Texas A&M
1940 Tom Harmon, Michigan	Tom Harmon, Michigan
1941 Bruce Smith, Minnesota	Jack Crain, Texas
1942 Frank Sinkwich, Georgia	Frank Sinkwich, Georgia
1943 Angelo Bertelli, Notre Dame	Bob Odell, Penn
1944 Les Horvath, Ohio State	Glenn Davis, Army
1945 Doc Blanchard, Army	Doc Blanchard, Army

1946 Glenn Davis, Army . . . . .Charlie Trippi, Georgia
1947 Johnny Lujack, Notre Dame . . . . .Doak Walker, SMU
1948 Doak Walker, SMU . . . . .Doak Walker, SMU
1949 Leon Hart, Notre Dame . . . . .Charlie Justice, North Carolina
1950 Vic Janowicz, Ohio State . . . . .Kyle Rote, SMU
1951 Dick Kazmaier, Princeton . . . . .Hank Lauricella, Tennessee
1952 Billy Vessels, Oklahoma . . . . .Billy Vessels, Oklahoma
1953 John Lattner, Notre Dame . . . . .Paul Cameron, UCLA
1954 Alan Ameche, Wisconsin . . . . .Dicky Maegle, Rice
1955 Howard Cassady, Ohio State . . . . .Jim Swink, TCU
1956 Paul Hornung, Notre Dame . . . . .Jim Brown, Syracuse
1957 John David Crow, Texas A&M . . . . . . .John David Crow, Texas A&M
1958 Pete Dawkins, Army . . . . .Pete Dawkins, Army
1959 Billy Cannon, LSU . . . . .Billy Cannon, LSU
1960 Joe Bellino, Navy . . . . .Jake Gibbs, Mississippi
1961 Ernie Davis, Syracuse . . . . .James Saxton, Texas
1962 Terry Baker, Oregon State .Jerry Stovall, LSU
1963 Roger Staubach, Navy . . . . .Roger Staubach, Navy
1964 John Huarte, Notre Dame . . . . .Tommy Nobis, Texas
1965 Mike Garrett, USC . . . . .Donny Anderson, Texas Tech
1966 Steve Spurrier, Florida . . . . .Bob Griese, Purdue
1967 Gary Beban, UCLA . . . . .Gary Beban, UCLA
1968 O.J. Simpson, USC . . . . .O.J. Simpson, USC
1969 Steve Owens, Oklahoma . . . . .James Street, Texas
1970 Jim Plunkett, Stanford .Jim Plunkett, Stanford
1971 Pat Sullivan, Auburn . . . . .Jack Mildren, Oklahoma
1972 Johnny Rodgers, Nebraska . . . . .Johnny Rodgers, Nebraska
1973 John Cappelletti, Penn State . . . . .Roosevelt Leaks, Texas
1974 Archie Griffin, Ohio State . . . . .Joe Washington, Oklahoma
1975 Archie Griffin, Ohio State . . . . .Archie Griffin, Ohio State
1976 Tony Dorsett, Pitt . . . . .Tony Dorsett, Pitt
1977 Earl Campbell, Texas . . . . .Earl Campbell, Texas
1978 Billy Sims, Oklahoma .Billy Sims, Oklahoma
1979 Charles White, USC . . . . .Charles White, USC
1980 George Rogers, South Carolina . . . . .Herschel Walker, Georgia
1981 Marcus Allen, USC . . . . .Marcus Allen, USC
1982 Herschel Walker, Georgia . . . . .Eric Dickerson, SMU
1983 Mike Rozier, Nebraska .Turner Gill, Nebraska
1984 Doug Flutie, Boston College . . . . .Doug Flutie, Boston College
1985 Bo Jackson, Auburn . . . . .Chuck Long, Iowa
1986 Vinny Testaverde, Miami . . . . .Vinny Testaverde, Miami
1987 Tim Brown, Notre Dame . . . . .Don McPherson, Syracuse
1988 Barry Sanders, Oklahoma State . . . . . . .Barry Sanders, Oklahoma State
1989 Andre Ware, Houston . . . . .Andre Ware, Houston
1990 Ty Detmer, Brigham Young . . . . .Darren Lewis, Texas A&M
1991 Desmond Howard, Michigan . . . . .Desmond Howard, Michigan

1992 Gino Torretta, Miami . . . . .Marshall Faulk, San Diego St.
1993 Charlie Ward, Florida State . . . . .Charlie Ward, Florida State
1994 Rashaan Salaam, Colorado . . . . .Ki-Jana Carter, Penn State
1995 Eddie George, Ohio State . . . . .Tommie Frazier, Nebraska
1996 Danny Wuerffel, Florida . . . . .Jake Plummer, Arizona State
1997 Charles Woodson, Michigan. . . . . .Peyton Manning, Tennessee
1998 Ricky Williams, Texas . . . .**Ricky Williams, Texas**

Here comes Lewis off the bench . . .

. . . and down goes Moegle, but it's a 95-yard TD.

"Dicky Maegle that good?" Tommy Earl asked.

"When he had an 'o' in his name," I said.

That required an explanation. Dicky Maegle was Dicky Moegle ... M-o-e-g-l-e ... with an 'o' ... when he did all that terrific stuff at Rice. When he was the darting halfback who teamed up with the All-America fullback Kosse Johnson to lead Rice to the conference title in '53 and romped for those amazing 265 yards in the Cotton Bowl game against Alabama, which was when he suffered the infamous off-the-bench tackle by Tommy Lewis. When a year later, in '54, he gained more than 900 yards, did the punting, played great defense, and led the nation in punt returns while carrying a now so-so Rice team to a 7-3 record — and would have won the Heisman if the voters had been as smart as me.

Moegle officially took the 'o' out of his name and put in the 'a' later in life for reasons that were clear only to him. Probably figured it would go better with the pronunciation. Maygle was the way you were supposed to say it all along.

Dashing Dickey, old 47

Your typist is pleased to say he was among those in the Cotton Bowl that afternoon when the Alabama guy came off the bench to tackle Moegle. Again, I saw it with my own eyes when Tommy Lewis entered his name into notorious football lore.

None of us upstairs in the press box knew exactly where he'd come from, and TV didn't have replays in those days. All we saw was a Moegle on his way to a 95-yard touchdown run on a sweep to the right when suddenly around midfield he was smacked down by something that might have fallen out of the sky.

Then we noticed the red Alabama jersey quickly crawl out from under Moegle and scoot back to the sideline. And while that was happening, referee Cliff Shaw threw up his arms and signaled a touchdown.

Alabama was the Southeastern Conference champion, quarterbacked by a fellow named Bart Starr, and had grabbed a 6-0 lead in the first quarter. In the second quarter Moegle had already cut and side-stepped and sprinted 79 yards for the touchdown that put Rice up 7 to 6. For almost a whole quarter, it was the longest TD run in Cotton Bowl history.

Then Moegle went on that journey in the second period.

It was in the third quarter that Moegle skittered 34 yards for his third touchdown of the day, the score that insured Rice's 28-to-6 victory.

Try this stat on, see how it fits: Moegle averaged 24.1 yards per carry in his 11 gallops for the 265 yards on the afternoon. It's still the greatest rushing performance in bowl history.

While there's photographic evidence that I was on the scene that day, in the locker room with Moegle after the game, I can't remember exactly what he tried to tell reporters, or sketch with the pad and pen I'd given him. Maybe he was just asking me if I was old enough to vote.

It ought to be said that the guy who put me there that day was Blackie Sherrod,

By BLACKIE SHERROD

Dallas Times Herald Sports Editor

KINGS ISLAND, O., Aug. 6, 1980 — The stain is unfortunate, but permanent. It's like an unsightly birthmark on a beautiful woman, a blemish which becomes more noticeable as the lady grows older until that is ALL you see.

Dicky Maegle wishes he had never heard of Tommy Lewis, that there was no such impulsive bungler. THEN maybe the college football researchers would record that Jan. 1, 1954, with proper respect for what it was — the greatest offensive show in a major bowl game.

Instead Maegle finds he is remembered mainly for a freakish goof in which he was the innocent victim.

Wrong Way Roy Riegels, too, is branded in memory for a boner in a bowl game. But this was Riegels' doing, nobody's fault but his. In comparison, Maegle was a bystander struck by the bandit's getaway car.

There he was, galloping along in wide open spaces of the Cotton Bowl, minding his own business en route to his second long-range touchdown of the second quarter, when an Alabama highwayman burst from the ambush of his own bench, ran on the field and cracked Maegle with a blindside collision that COULD have crushed the Owl halfback like a sopaipilla.

Then this Tommy Lewis, the skulking trespasser, rushed back to the bench, sat down, buried his head in his hands and started crying. He didn't even look to see if Maegle was in two pieces or more. There are folks doing three to five in the state joint for less.

And now when Maegle was inducted into the College Hall of Fame here this week, the conversation centered around Lewis & Maegle, rather than Dick as a solo act. He didn't especially giggle over it.

Some Southwest graybeards remember the Ed Sullivan blotch of the event. Sullivan had the biggest TV show of the time, a variety show on Sunday night, and he loved to introduce figures in current news from his stage and in the audience.

The nation was abuzz over Lewis' illegal tackle, which was featured over and over on the national toob. The game was on Friday. Sullivan called Maegle, his coach Jess Neely, and Lewis and wanted them for his show.

"Coach Neely was already in New York for a meeting," Maegle recalled. "This was in the days of prop planes, and I flew seven hours from Houston to New York, two or three stops. I went straight to the theater that afternoon for rehearsal.

"Backstage there was all this confusion. There were guys juggling all over the place, and other guys turning flips. I remember a bear standing on a ball. I never said anything to anybody, and nobody said anything to me."

On the live television show, Ed Sullivan called Lewis, Maegle, and Neely on the stage and introduced them. Then he talked to Lewis only, and asked him why he'd done what he did.

In his thick Southern accent, Lewis said, "Why, Mistuh Sullivan, ah gess ah wuz jist so full of Alabama."

Sullivan then turned to the audience and said, "Let's hear it for this fine young American," and everybody cheered like Tommy Lewis had just rescued the U.S.S. Pueblo. Maegle and Neely were asked no questions, and never uttered a word.

After the show Sullivan thanked the boys and told them they had a fine room waiting for them at the Waldorf.

Maegle waited a while before he went over to Sullivan and said, "I don't want this to sound wrong, but would you mind if I got my own room?"

Sullivan looked surprised, but then Maegle said, "Just two days ago, this guy came off the sideline and knocked me out in front of all those people, and now he's on national television. You can't tell what he might do if he woke up in the middle of the night. He might throw me out the window."

Sullivan stared, then snapped his fingers, and said, "Get this boy a room of his own!"

Maegle returned for a big senior season in which he led the Southwest in rushing and scoring and led the nation in punt returns, and gained consensus All-America. And then he went to a seven-year career as a defensive back in the NFL.

But this week, as he became the 24th Southwest Conference player to be recognized by the Hall of Fame, Maegle found some things stay the same for a quarter-century. Like conversation topics.

the *Fort Worth Press* and *Dallas Times Herald*, the man who hired me for the first two of the only four jobs I've ever had.

Twenty-five years after the fact, there was an occasion when Dicky Moegle, or Maegle, was inducted into the College Football Hall of Fame, and Blackie was present.

Of course, all those years ago — and on deadline in the Cotton Bowl press box — Blackie probably made the best statement of all about the shocking incident. He wrote in the old *Fort Worth Press* how there was one thing that might have proved even more embarrassing for Tommy Lewis.

Lewis could have jumped off the bench, run onto the field, and Moegle could have stiff-armed him and continued merrily on his 95-yard way.

THEY MADE THE SWC EXCITING

Baylor's Larry Isbell

Jack Spikes, TCU

Donny Anderson, Texas Tech

Bob Smith, A&M

TCU's Sonny Gibbs

"Dandy" Don Meredith

Arkansas' Lance Alworth

A&M's Darren Lewis

TCU's Kenneth Davis

SMU's Eric Dickerson

Ronnie Bull
of Baylor

Tommy Kramer of Rice

THIRTEEN

I F THERE was anything as big as the Maegle-Lewis thing in the Southwest during the 1950s, it was the conflict that came to be known as "The Hurricane Game."

Where were you on Oct. 20, 1956?

Did you go to that school, buddy?

If you were a semi-adult by then and cared anything at all about Texas A&M or TCU, you should have been crammed into Kyle Field in College Station, Texas, on that day.

The game figured to be — and was — one of the fiercest, wildest, bloodiest, most baroque Poll Bowls ever played.

It enjoyed an outrageous buildup, like for 12 months.

The Frogs had a revenge factor going for them. A narrow 19-to-16 upset at the hands of the same Aggies was the only blot on their record in '55 as they flattened all other opponents behind the audacious, breakaway running of Jim Swink, the greatest halfback in TCU history. In all likelihood that upset cost TCU the national championship. With a 9-1 record, the Frogs couldn't out-poll Oklahoma and Maryland, the two undefeated teams in '55, but comparative scores against common foes and TCU's much tougher schedule would have favored the Frogs in the voting over the Sooners and Terps — if only they hadn't let that A&M game slip away.

Now both teams were back, loaded again with most of the same gifted athletes from '55, undefeated and ranked among the nation's Top 10, the Frogs fourth, the Aggies seventh. Their game-time records:

TCU (3-0)			TEXAS A&M (3-0-1)		
32	Kansas	0	19	Villanova	0
41	Arkansas	6	9	LSU	6
23	Alabama	6	40	Texas Tech	7
			14	Houston	14

TCU's more passionate fans saw the game as a case of Good vs. Evil, the Aggies being on NCAA probation for recruiting violations — for bringing in some of those studs who'd helped knock the Frogs off the year before. Under the curious probation, the Aggies were eligible for the conference championship but ineligible to play in a bowl game.

Somewhere in the pile up is Jim Swink, with or without a TCU touchdown.

Don Watson's controversial interception in the making. He's in dark jersey.

John David Crow skirts end in second-half "dry" jersey, different numeral.

Jim Swink waged another halfback duel in Cotton Bowl with Syracuse immortal Jim Brown (44).

That aside, the teams were alarmingly different on the field, as different as the two lavishly headlined backs who took the field that day.

TCU's Jim Swink was a gliding, side-stepping, bounce-off, long-distance threat. John David Crow was a barging, bruising, punishing runner.

TCU's coach, the folksy Abe Martin, once said to me of Swink, "Aw, he's just a little old rubber-legged outfit nobody can catch."

After John David won the Heisman in '57, there was a moment when a sportswriter pointed out to Bear Bryant, the A&M coach, that Crow had only gained 562 yards from scrimmage, and that didn't seem like very many yards for a Heisman Trophy winner.

To which the Bear said, "That don't count all the people he knocked down."

The Frogs were a sleek, pass-run, offense-minded machine coached by the kindly Martin, "the Jacksboro Philosopher." Most of the more prominent Aggies were survivors of the iron-fisted Bryant's Junction, Texas, "death camp." Overall, they were a spirited, defense-minded bunch.

Bear had brought pursuit to the Southwest Conference. Pursuit was the word he gave to a swarming, gang-tackling, spearing, sticking defense.

Gnawing on his cigar, Abe Martin would say, "Everybody's talkin' about pursuit. Hell, that ain't nothin' but chase 'em and catch 'em."

Going into the game, both coaches knew TCU had a more varied attack. To go along with Swink, the Frogs had an all-conference quarterback, a talented thrower, in quarterback Chuck Curtis, and Abe Martin said, "We're gonna see if the Aggies can cover the whole field."

Bryant said of the Frogs: "They play like pros. You can't let 'em get too far ahead, they'll run you out of the stadium."

The lineups at the kickoff, when the sun was still shining:

TCU		TEXAS A&M
John Nikkel	LE	Gene Stallings
Norm Hamilton	LT	Charlie Krueger
John Groom	LG	Dennis Goehring
Joe Williams	C	Lloyd Hale
Vernon Uecker	RG	Dee Powell
Don Cooper	RT	Bobby Lockett
O'Day Williams	RE	John Tracey
Chuck Curtis	Q	Roddy Osborne
Jim Swink	LH	John David Crow
Ken Wineburg	RH	Loyd Taylor
Buddy Dike	F	Jack Pardee

Here's John David Crow on his way to the Heisman in 1957 action against Rice.

Happily, most of us of the sportswriting bent were in the warmth and comfort of the Kyle Field press box when the sky suddenly turned darker than an Aggie's maroon jersey, the light poles started to flap like palm trees, and here came the rain, hail, and wind to hammer the entire first half.

But without further ado, here's how it was seen that day by a 30-year veteran of Southwest Conference wars:

By FLEM HALL

Fort Worth Star-Telegram Sports Editor

COLLEGE STATION, Oct. 20 — By the margin of Loyd Taylor's extra-point kick after a fourth quarter touchdown, the Texas A&M Aggies toppled TCU by a score of 7-6 here this storm-tossed Saturday afternoon in a blood and thunder football game that started before a capacity crowd of 42,000 and finished with about half that many drenched spectators in the Kyle Field stands.

Winds up to an estimated 90 miles an hour and a downpour of rain handicapped both teams throughout the first half, which was scoreless.

The Aggies threw only one pass during the wet, slippery afternoon, but it was good for their lone touchdown.

The TCU Frogs, who had figuratively hung on the lip of the scoring cup throughout the near hurricane, took the lead in the third quarter when O'Day Williams made a one-handed grab in the end zone of a 12-yard Chuck Curtis pass to cap a drive from midfield.

Harold Pollard's placekick for the extra point popped up a bit wide of the south goal posts.

It was a frustrating day all around for the Frogs. They had one touchdown called back by an offside penalty. They were denied another touchdown when an official ruled Jim Swink was stopped an inch from the goal at the peak of the storm. They missed two field goal attempts and they suffered a crippling interception just when they were rolling at the Aggie 18 toward a put-away score in the final period.

TCU threatened seven times and scored only once. Other drives were stopped at the one-inch line, the 2-, 16-, 20-, 24-, and 18-yard lines of the stubborn Aggies.

The big hero for A&M was Don Watson, the senior reserve halfback from Franklin, who killed the Frogs last year with his fourth quarter 51-yard touchdown run.

First, Watson got the ball for the Aggies by making a leaping interception in his own end zone of a Chuck Curtis pass that was almost in the hands of Jim Shofner. The catch was made so close to the sideline, the Frogs argued heatedly that it shouldn't have counted. But it did.

From their own 20, then, with only 10 minutes left in the game, the Aggies went on their winning 80-yard drive.

John David Crow struck first with a bruising 21-yard run around his right end.

Quarterback Roddy Osborne kept for two yards.

Next, Watson went spinning through the middle and fought and stumbled his way for 37 yards to the TCU 20.

Crow powered for two, then swept right end again for 11 huge yards. TCU momentarily stiffened, holding Osborne's two keepers for a net loss of one yard.

Jim Swink averaged a record 8.2 yards per carry in his near-Heisman season of 1955.

It was then third down from the eight when Watson took a handoff, ran to his left, then suddenly flipped a pass to Crow, who was running free in the end zone. Taylor then hurried into the game and with Watson holding, booted the ball through for the vital extra point.

The game began with TCU trying to beat the gathering storm — there were tornado warnings before the opening kickoff. The Frogs moved effectively with runs and passes for 63 yards but the drive stalled at the Aggie 26, shy of a first down by inches.

Their best drive carried 73 yards through the rain and wind as Curtis and Swink struck from Abe Martin's new spread-T formation — put in for these Aggies — which sent Bear Bryant scrambling to a slate on the sideline to draw up a defense for it.

Swink scored from the three, but offsides was called, and four plays later, Ken Wineburg lost the ball on a fumble, which John Tracey recovered for the Aggies. There was no better lineman on the field all day than Tracey, unless it was TCU's tackle, Norman Hamilton.

A rash of fumbles broke out in the storm-darkened second quarter, and Hamilton recovered one of them at the A&M eight. Swink quickly slashed for five yards, then appeared to score from the three, but the ball was placed at the one-foot line. Twice more as the wind howled out of the black sky and hail pounded, Swink appeared to plow through to the end zone, but even though one official signaled a touchdown on the fourth down dive, another official overruled and put the ball at the one-inch line.

For most of the day, it looked as if the Frogs were "in" as the winner, but finally another storm hit them — a maroon-shirted Aggie storm.

Post-hurricane postscripts:

★ The Aggies faced another tough opponent the following Saturday in an undefeated Baylor team that had a line anchored by the All-America guard Bill Glass and a backfield that could call on the fleet Del Shofner for assorted duties. But A&M unleashed John David Crow in the fourth quarter and fashioned yet another late drive to win 19 to 13.

This was a Baylor team that also lost to TCU by 7 to 6 but wound up with an 8-2 record, which put the Bears in the Sugar Bowl. There, by the score of 13 to 7 they upset an unbeaten and No. 2-ranked Tennessee team that had All-America Johnny Majors at tailback.

On that same day, TCU was in the Cotton Bowl as the Southwest Conference representative instead of the probation-plagued Aggies, and the Frogs did quite nicely. With Chuck Curtis throwing perfect strikes and Jim Swink getting off some of his final cuts and dashes — and in a contest that wasn't really as close as the score suggests — the Frogs handled Syracuse and the incomparable Jim Brown by 28 to 27.

The saga of the '56 season ended after the bowl games with the Aggies at 9-0-1 and Oklahoma at 10-0 as the nation's only undefeated teams, but the Sooners scooped all the No. 1 honors — and they could probably thank Bear Bryant for that in part.

Here's why: in their earlier 14-14 tie with the University of Houston, then the power of the Missouri Valley Conference, it was Bear who refused to order a field goal in the final moments when the Aggies were on the Cougars' goal. Instead, A&M tried four running plays that were stopped short of the end zone.

Explaining his decision afterward, Bear said, "If you can't make one damn yard, you don't deserve to win."

Looking back on it, that victory would have left the Aggies with the same perfect record as Oklahoma, and the pollsters might have given some thought to the fact that A&M had waded through a far tougher schedule. The Aggies played five teams with winning records while the Sooners played only one. Moreover, A&M's 10 foes that season won a total of 49 games while Oklahoma's won only 32.

Surely, any reasonable voter ...

★ Yeah, well, eat your heart out, Aggies. That was the attitude of TCU's loyalists, who to this day, more than 40 years later, choose to think a crew of incompetent zebras stole "the Hurricane Game" from them.

You can still hear the complaints ... Nobody was offsides when Swink scored the first touchdown, it should have counted ...Wineburg was down, it shouldn't have been ruled a fumble ... Watson was out of bounds on the interception ... Swink scored at least twice in the middle of the storm ...

Only a few moments ago, Buddy Dike, TCU's underrated fullback, the antidote to A&M's All-America Jack Pardee, was saying, "I led the play through the hole on one of Jim's runs. I wound up in the end zone and Swink was lying on top of me, clutching my jersey. The official closest to the play called it a touchdown, but another one came running over — rain splattering on his glasses — and said no score."

Even today Chuck Curtis thinks he could have removed any doubt about the final result if he'd called an audible at the line of scrimmage and run a bootleg keeper. The Aggies were stacked to stop Swink.

"I could have walked in," he recalled. "But I was afraid to change the play. The hail was bouncing off our helmets so hard, nobody could have heard me."

★The temptation is too great not to share a press box moment with you from that day.

Like most big-city dailies in Texas, the *Fort Worth Press* was on hand to cover the game with a cluster of poets. Blackie Sherrod, our leader, was there along with myself, Bud Shrake, Jerre Todd, and a tall young part-timer named Jim Hendricks. Except for Blackie, the rest of us were all TCU grads, some caring more deeply about the outcome than others.

As the last seconds of the game were ticking off — A&M assured of victory — we already knew our assignments. Blackie would do this, I would do that, Shrake would do something else, Todd would catch the Aggie locker room, Hendricks would go to TCU's.

We were all sort of standing there when Blackie said to Todd and Hendricks, "You better get started downstairs."

"I can't," Hendricks said.

Blackie looked at him. We all looked at him.

"I can't go see those guys," Hendricks confessed limply. "It's too sad. They'll be heartbroken."

"You what?" said Blackie with a glare, one that insinuated this was journalism, for Christ's sake.

Hendricks defiantly said, "You didn't go to that school, buddy!"

The rest of us were stunned. Nobody, especially a young rookie, spoke like that to Blackie Sherrod, the Capo tutti da capos.

Suddenly, then, we were more amused by the incident than stunned, being cynics. And led by the major lyricist, Jerre Todd, right there in the press box, we burst into a song we made up as we went along. We sang:

You didn't go to that school, buddy.
You never lived in Tom Brown Hall.
You ain't had no dealings with Chancellor Sadler,
You never been to the Howdy Week Ball.

Todd, I recall, kind of danced around as we warbled through it. Blackie could only collapse in laughter. Jim Hendricks, I should mention, went on to become a successful magazine editor in New York.

The song still lives. We sing it at certain gatherings, but only after the appropriate number of cocktails.

FOURTEEN

T.J. LAMBERT wondered how often sportswriters break into song in press boxes.

"That day in College Station is the only occasion I know of in football," I said. "It's possible it happens at figure skating, but that's just a guess on my part."

T.J. said, "You'd think there'd be more of it today, what with so many girls writing stories."

Billy Clyde grinned, looking at T.J. "You think there'd be more singing in press boxes because there are more girl sportswriters around?"

T.J. shrugged.

Billy Clyde said, "I hope that doesn't get back to Gloria Steinem."

Tommy Earl Bruner made a confession. He was a girl-sportswriter groupie. Said he used to be a woman-news-anchor groupie, but they worried too much about their hair. He was a girl-sportswriter groupie now. It stood to reason most of them had loose morals or they wouldn't be in the business.

"I got one stopping by tonight," he said. "Cindy ought to be here in a minute. She had to write something about the game."

Surprised, T.J. said, "You talking about Cindy Pritchard with the *Fort Worth Light & Shopper*? She's coming here?"

"Good writer," Tommy Earl said. "And hung."

"She know you're married?" T.J. asked.

"That's what she likes best about me. But I ought to be married to a woman sportswriter, don't you think? Get game tickets, go on good trips. She'd have to work a lot of nights, I'd have free time to jack around."

"Read a lot of women sportswriters, do you?" said Billy Clyde.

Tommy Earl said, "Depends on what they write. Nobody reads any sportswriter if they write about the NBA. I wouldn't read Cindy if she wrote about the armpits. Some Zulu makes a layup, two Swahilis miss free throws. End of story."

"What if she wrote ice hockey?" I inquired.

Tommy Earl said, "Nobody reads hockey either. There's a great game. Bunch of guys with no teeth speaking Ukrainian, playing for Dallas and Miami. Uniforms look like the way everybody dresses in Duluth."

"Nobody's ever seen a goal," T.J. said.

"Nobody wants to see a goal," said Tommy Earl. "All hockey fans want to see are the silly sumbitches gettin' slammed into walls and their eyeballs gettin' poked out with sticks."

"So T.E., what do you like about soccer, other than soccer moms?" Billy Clyde asked playfully.

"That's about it," Tommy Earl said. "I'll tell you the best thing about your soccer moms. On an average day, there ain't no soccer dads around. All you do is hang in, look interested, and cull."

Somebody brought up track and field, saying it used to be important but now that's only true in an Olympic year. T.J. said he couldn't remember the last time he'd read a track and field story, but he was sure it had something to do with steroids. Tommy Earl was a big fan of the sport. He said, "I'd rather catch my grandmother naked than see my son win cross-country."

Since Jim Tom Pinch wasn't with us — there was a journalistic conflict of some kind that required him to be in Zurich — everyone turned to me for an opinion about sportswriters today.

I said there were a lot of good young ones around everywhere, like Cindy Pritchard. But the problem with too many of them now, they want to be Woodstein and Bernford. They want to go out and find a college running back who let somebody buy him an illegal cheeseburger eight months ago, or find some poor old assistant coach who made the mistake of casually saying a majorette was a good-looking babe.

They write those stories, and nobody gives a hoot about them, but TV picks them up, blabs about it for three days, and finally causes the running back and the assistant coach to be sent to prison for the rest of their lives.

No Pulitzers for anybody, just some shit to stir up the politically correct Nazis and professors who don't have tenure yet.

Depressing, I said. All in all, I'd rather talk about yesteryear.

MORE GREAT SWC LINEMEN

A&M's Charley Krueger

Baylor's Bill Glass

Mike Singletary of Baylor

Arkansas' Loyd Phillips

Darrell Lester, TCU's two-year
All-America center

E.J. Holub, Texas Tech

TCU's Don Floyd

Wilson Whitley, Houston

Texas' Bud McFadin

SMU's J.C. (Ironman) Wetsel

FIFTEEN

THAT'S WHAT everybody was afraid of. Undaunted, however, I pressed on into the Sixties, trudging toward the last great Poll Bowl in the Southwest Conference. You could make the case that where the conference was concerned, the Sixties rivaled the Thirties for goldenness.

It was the decade in which Texas' Darrell Royal and Arkansas' Frank Broyles achieved sainthood, producing six national champions in the years from 1961 through 1970 — five for Royal, one for Broyles.

In their 20-year reign, from 1958 through 1976, Darrell won or tied for 11 conference championships while Frank won or tied for seven. It's a short list of coaches who seized any title or piece of one over the same span. Those dogged gentlemen were TCU's Abe Martin (1958-59), SMU's Hayden Fry (1966), Texas A&M's Gene Stallings (1967), Baylor's Grant Teaff (1974), A&M's Emory Bellard (1975), and Houston's Bill Yeoman and Texas Tech's Steve Sloan, who shared the crown in '76.

The impact that Royal and Broyles had on the conference brings to mind how hard it is for a school to replace a saint. Texas' has hired four coaches since Royal — Fred Akers, David McWilliams, John Mackovic, and Mack Brown. Arkansas has hired six since Broyles — Lou Holtz, Ken Hatfield, Jack Crowe, Joe Kines, Danny Ford, and Houston Nutt.

Some of those fellows won conference championships themselves, but obviously they didn't do it often enough to satisfy the alumni.

Replacing a St. Darrell has always been a problem in college football, and all of the other SWC schools suffered from the same rash.

Fodder for trivia junkies:

Who were the two coaches Texas A&M employed after Homer Norton retired in '47? Harry Stiteler and Ray George.

Who were the seven who've held the job since the Aggies went looking for another Bear Bryant in '58? Jim Myers, Hank Foldberg, Gene Stallings, Emory Bellard, Tom Wilson, Jackie Sherrill, and R.C. Slocum.

Who are the eight guys TCU has hired since Abe Martin retired in '66? Fred Taylor, Jim Pittman, Billy Tohill, Jim Shofner, F.A. Dry, Jim Wacker, Pat Suillivan, and Dennis Franchione.

Rice tried nine character-builders between Jess Neely's retirement in '66 and Ken Hatfield's arrival in '94. In order of their brief appearances, they were Bo Hagan,

Bill Peterson, Al Conover, Homer Rice, Ray Alborn, Watson Brown, Jerry Berndt, and Fred Goldsmith.

Since Matty Bell hung it up after the '49 season, SMU has gone through...how many? Ten. Rusty Russell, Woody Woodard, Bill Meek, Hayden Fry, Dave Smith, Ron Meyer, Bobby Collins, Forrest Gregg, Tom Rossley, and Mike Cavan.

How many head men has Texas Tech given the job since DeWitt Weaver lobbied the Red Raiders into the conference in '60 before stepping aside? Well, let's see. JT King, Jim Carlen, Steve Sloan, Rex Dockery, Jerry Moore, David McWilliams, and Spike Dykes.

After Houston's Bill Yeoman hung it up in '86, the Cougars have gone with Jack Pardee, John Jenkins, and Kim Helton.

Baylor's off to a good start. Grant Teaff retired in '92, but since then the Bears have dumped two, Chuck Reedy and Dave Roberts, and were going with Kevin Steele the last time I looked.

But over the 80-year history of the SWC, there've been some success stories. Here's the list of men who managed to win two or more SWC titles:

DARRELL ROYAL — Texas 11
DANA X. BIBLE — Texas A&M, Texas 8
FRANK BROYLES — Arkansas 7
MATTY BELL — SMU 4
JESS NEELY — Rice 4
BILL YEOMAN — Houston 4
DUTCH MEYER — TCU 3
HOMER NORTON — Texas A&M 3
RAY MORRISON — SMU 3
ABE MARTIN — TCU 3
JACKIE SHERRILL — Texas A&M 3
R.C. SLOCUM — Texas A&M 3
KEN HATFIELD — Arkansas, Rice 3
FRANCIS SCHMIDT — TCU 2
JIMMY KITTS — Rice 2
CLYDE LITTLEFIELD — Texas 2
FRANK BRIDGES — Baylor 2
ED PRICE — Texas 2
BOBBY COLLINS — SMU 2
GRANT TEAFF — Baylor 2
FRED AKERS — Texas 2
JOHN MACKOVIC — Texas 2

You have to go to your research to find very many coaches who won more major conference championships than Royal did at Texas. You'll come up with Alabama's Bear Bryant in the SEC, Ohio State's Woody Hayes in the Big 10, and

THE TALENTED LONGHORNS OF 1961

Tackle Don Talbert

Halfback Jack Collins

All-America halfback
James Saxton

Linebacker Pat Culpepper

Quarterback Mike Cotten

Alabama's Bear Bryant in the SEC, Ohio State's Woody Hayes in the Big 10, and Oklahoma's Bud Wilkinson and Barry Switzer in the Big Eight, then you'll go blind.

Ironically, Darrell was a halfback, Split-T quarterback, and All-America defensive back at OU from '46 through '49, which means he helped Bud win four of his 14 Big Eight titles.

The Royal-Broyles Sixties also saw the conference turn out more All-Americans than it did in any other decade, a total of 43. Among the non-dropout, no-protest Sixties heroes were Lance (Bambi) Alworth, the fastest man at Arkansas since Clyde (Smackover) Scott in the late Forties, Donny Anderson, "the Golden Palomino," at Texas Tech, and before him, E. J. (The Beast) Holub. There were James (Slick) Street and Steve (Woo Woo) Worster at Texas, Baylor's Ronnie (No) Bull, and SMU's Jerry ("Fly by Us") Levias, the fiery little flanker who integrated the league.

But more important, the Sixties unleashed Texas' Tommy Nobis and TCU's Bob Lilly, two honest legends who continue to make college football's All-Time Team every time people get around to picking one.

The last one I saw was in the early Nineties when some 300 writers and broadcasters around the country were asked to pick college football's all-time squad of 22. From the Southwest Conference, Nobis and Lilly made it along with Sam Baugh and Doak Walker.

If this says that Nobis, Lilly, Baugh, and Walker were the four greatest players in SWC history, I think I can live with it. I might add that TCU, Alabama, and Southern Cal were the only three schools to have more than one player named to the team — and I'd like some credit for not shouting that out loud, if you don't mind.

Lilly, who became an All-America tackle for TCU in 1960, had been recruited out of Throckmorton, Texas, by a postcard from Abe Martin. Try that today on a wanted high-school athlete. You might write the postcard, but you better take a fully equipped Range Rover with you — and a job for his daddy — when you go to visit him.

Before Lilly acquired All-America stature, he gained some notoriety for lifting up a car by himself so a TCU friend, who didn't have a jack, could change a tire.

"It was just a little Renault," Bob explained modestly.

Abe, in his quaint way, once said of Lilly, "He's just a big old green pea, but he'll stand in there for you like a picket fence."

Lilly's nickname was "The Purple Cloud," not "The Picket Fence" or "The Green Pea," in the days when he gathered up and threw away ballcarriers for the Frogs. Then he became part of the "Doomsday Defense" when he picked up and threw-away ballcarriers for the Dallas Cowboys.

Nobis made All-America as a linebacker/guard for Royal in '64 and '65. He was a fearsome competitor who appeared on the covers of both *Sports Illustrated* and *Life* before he shucked his burnt-orange jersey.

He epitomized the kind of player Darrell Royal loved. "One of those pigs who'll jump right in the slop for you," as the coach liked to put it.

Curiously, Nobis's best season may have been in '63 when he was a sophomore starter on the undefeated, untied national champions. There were many superstars on that team — quarterback Duke Carlisle, halfback Tommy Ford, tackle Scott

THE AWESOME LONGHORNS OF 1963

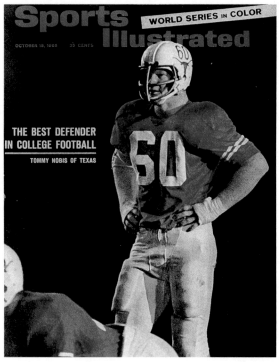

All-timer Tommy Nobis

Quarterback Duke Carlisle

All-Americans Tommy Ford and Scott
Appleton

Halfback Phil Harris

He all but undressed Roger Staubach, the Heisman winner, when the No. 1
Longhorns slaughtered No. 2 Navy by 28 to 6 in the Cotton Bowl. It was after
that bowl game that a Navy lineman was asked if he'd like another shot at Texas.
"Not if that Nobis guy is gonna play," the Middie said.

It was also after that Cotton Bowl game, and after studying numerous Texas game films, that Army Coach Paul Dietzel, who'd left LSU to take over at West Point, said, "Tommy Nobis is not only the greatest linebacker I've ever seen, he's the greatest linebacker who ever lived!"

It was a violent competitor like Nobis who probably inspired Royal to remark for posterity, "Talk about X's and O's all you want to, but football games are won by angry people."

Darrell Royal and Frank Broyles dolled up the national college landscape like few other coaching rivalries. They collided six times from '59 through '69 with perfect-record teams — spirited, quick-hitting outfits — that were serious contenders for the ultimate bumper sticker.

The Big Shootout was what the first game was labeled by whatever sportswriter wrote it and never got credit for it. The label caught on and the game kept on being called that, right up to the biggest-shootingest-outest contest of them all, in 1969.

You're talking to a typist who was fortunate enough to cover four of those heart-stoppers. There was Austin in '62 when Ernie Koy led a late drive that gave Texas a 7-to-3 win over Billy Moore & Co. There was Austin again in '64 when Ken Hatfield's thunderbolt punt return and Royal's failed 2-point gamble in the last seconds combined to give Arkansas a 14-to-13 win — and the national championship. And there was Fayetteville in '65 when the Razorbacks rolled up a 20-point lead, suddenly got overwhelmed by the Longhorns who regained the lead at 24-20, then came back themselves to win the game in the final moments by 27 to 24 on Jon Brittenum's passes to Bobby Crockett.

All that was terrific drama, worthy of Broadway, but it was summer stock compared to The Big Shootout of '69 — "The Game of the Century."

Television had long since moved the game from its usual mid-October date to December 6 in Fayetteville. It wasn't hard to know why. Virtually the same players were back from the shootout in '68 when Texas, behind the Wishbone magic of James Street, had won an exciting 39-to-29 victory.

Their season records at kickoff were enough to make everybody in Arkansas wear a pig for a hat, and everybody in Texas suffer from a terminal "hook 'em" sign.

TEXAS (9-0)			ARKANSAS (9-0)		
17	California	0	39	Oklahoma State	0
49	Texas Tech	7	55	Tulsa	0
56	Navy	17	24	TCU	6
27	Oklahoma	17	21	Baylor	7
31	Rice	0	52	Wichita State	14
45	SMU	14	35	Texas A&M	13
56	Baylor	14	30	Rice	6
69	TCU	7	28	SMU	15
49	Texas A&M	12	33	Texas Tech	0

Inasmuch as Texas was ranked No. 1 and Arkansas No. 2 in the nation, and this was the last game of the first 100 years of college football, it became the godfather of Poll Bowls.

Fayetteville was a madhouse all week. Signs were hung everywhere, from churches to convenience stores, imploring the Hogs to beat Texas and do various other things to Longhorns. My favorite: BEVO IS STERILE.

The excitement was compounded by the news that President Richard Nixon was coming and bringing with him his own national championship trophy that he'd present in the dressing room to the winning team.

This overshadowed the fact — certainly among atheists — that Rev. Billy Graham would also be in attendance.

As horns continually honked and music played from distances all around the stadium during Texas' final workout in Fayetteville on Friday, I'll always remember Darrell Royal starting to get his game-face on.

"Arkansas," he said, spitting. "What's it good for? All they do is sell jams and jellies by the side of the road."

Here were your regulars in the godfather of Poll Bowls:

OFFENSE

TEXAS		ARKANSAS
Cotton Speyrer	SE	Chuck Dicus
Bobby Wuensch	LT	Mike Kelson
Randy Stout	LG	Jerry Dossey
Forrest Wiegand	C	Rodney Brand
Mike Dean	RG	Ronnie Hammers
Bob McKay	RT	Bob Stankovich
Randy Peschel	TE	Pat Morrison
James Street	Q	Bill Montgomery
Jim Bertelsen	LH	Bill Burnett
Ted Koy	RH	Johnny Rees
Steve Worster	F	Bruce Maxwell

DEFENSE

Bill Atessis	LE	Bruce James
Greg Ploetz	LT	Roger Harnish
Carl White	RT	Dick Bumpas
David Arledge	RE	Rick Kersey
Bill Zapalac	LB	Lynn Garner
Glen Halsell	LB	Cliff Powell
Scott Henderson	LB	Mike Boschetti
Mike Campbell	DB	Bobby Field
Tom Campbell	DB	Terry Stewart
Danny Lester	DB	Jerry Moore
Freddy Steinmark	DB	Dennis Berner

The total number of All-Americans on the field that day — either current or future — was an incredible 13. Seven for Texas, six for Arkansas.

For Texas, there were Worster, Speyrer, McKay, Wuensch, Halsell, Atessis, and Henderson. For Arkansas, there were Dicus, Brand, Powell, James, Bumpas, and Bill McClard, the kicker.

THE IMMORTAL LONGHORNS OF 1967

Quarterback James Street

End Cotton Speyrer

Tackles Bobby Wuensch,
Bob McKay

Fullback Steve Worster

Halfbacks Ted Koy,
Jim Bertelsen

The winning touchdown for Texas.

Randy Peschel caught the pass that set up the game-winning touchdown for the Longhorns.

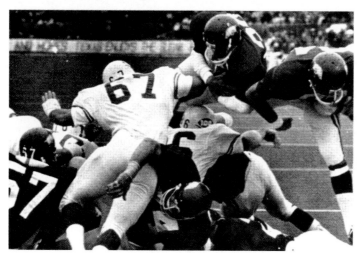

The game featured ferocious hitting.

Longhorns receive the President's Trophy.

As Poll Bowls go, it didn't measure up to some others. It certainly wasn't in a category with the 1971 Nebraska-Oklahoma game two years later — the Jack Mildren-Greg Pruitt vs. Johnny Rodgers-Rich Glover game — in which both teams more than lived up to advance notices.

The thought still lingers that the game might not have been as close on that crazy day in Fayetteville if Texas hadn't played poorly. The Longhorns committed six turnovers — four fumbles, two interceptions — and it took them three full quarters to shed their overconfidence.

After the game, the battle cry in the world's most crowded press box was, "It's too big for me." You heard such a battle cry often as a joke, but this time everybody meant it. Nobody wrote a prize-winner.

Therefore, that being the case, I suppose I might as well yield to my family's wishes and go with this deadline effort that mugged two armed guards, wrestled three editors to the floor, and sneaked into the pages of *Sports Illustrated*.

By DAN JENKINS

All week long in Texas the people said Hogs ain't nuthin' but groceries and that on Saturday, in the thundering zoo of Fayetteville, the No. 1 Longhorns would eat — to quote the most horrendous pun ever thought of by some Lone Star wit — "Hog meat with Worster-Speyrer sauce."

This is not exactly what Darrell Royal's team dined on up there in those maddening Ozark hills, of course. What Texas had was one hell of a hard time winning the national championship 15-14 from a quicker, more alert Arkansas team that for three quarters made the Longhorns look like your everyday, ordinary whip dog Baylor or Rice.

"We're beginning to develop some difficult fans," said Royal. "They don't understand there's no such person as King Kong, and when you start thinking there is, you can get ready to wipe your bloody nose."

For three quarters, Arkansas did practically all the bloodying. Bill Montgomery passed and ran the Longhorns into a state of shock and his own fans into the loudest afternoon ever. A furious Arkansas defense swarmed on Texas to cause four fumbles and two interceptions while Montgomery and his roommate-end, Chuck Dicus, combined for 14 points and what seemed like the safest lead since Orval Faubus rode in a motorcade.

"They're gonna come after us with their eyes pulled up like BBs," Royal warned. "And they'll defend every foot as if Frank has told 'em there's a 350-foot drop just behind 'em into a pile of rocks."

Arkansas certainly did that. Until the first play of the fourth quarter, the closest Texas had driven was to the Arkansas 31-yard line. The Razorbacks were doing exactly what Broyles said they had to do — stay put and don't miss tackles — in order to stop the second-best rushing team that ever played college football.

Meanwhile, the cool and clever Montgomery hurled a 21-yard pass to John Rees to set up a touchdown in the first quarter and a 29-yard touchdown to Dicus in the third.

Maybe Texas didn't panic because the Longhorns had been behind 14-0 before, back in October against an Oklahoma that was higher than your usual astronaut collecting gray rocks. And maybe Texas didn't panic because the Longhorns had James Street at quarterback.

Street is not an especially good passer, and he's never been compared to O.J. Simpson or even Jim Bertelsen in the open field, but James Street is a winner. He had never lost a game in 18 straight since becoming the Texas quarterback in the third game of last year.

So let's talk about the comeback, for that is all there is left that's important about this centennial year of the sport.

Upstairs in the chaos of the press box, which President Nixon had moved into at halftime, a very miserable man stood holding hands, for luck, with a pretty girl. He was Jones Ramsey, the Texas publicity man, and she was Barbara Specht, the Centennial Queen.

"I hate to be partial," said the queen, who goes to Texas Tech, "but after all, I am a Texan."

Ramsey moaned, "We're jinxed today, that's all."

About that time, on second down and nine from the Arkansas 42, Street, who bears the nickname Slick because of his good looks, flashy clothes, and ball-handling, dropped back to pass. Then, seeing his receivers covered, he darted through the line, flashed into the secondary, slipped past tacklers and sped on an angle across the field, running for either the goal line or the presidential helicopter. No one was about to catch him. It was a 42-yard touchdown run.

Street went for two points on the conversion, which wasn't so surprising. When you're No. 1 you have to try to stay that way. So Slick ran an option to his left and barged in. It was 14-8 now, and suddenly this was the Texas-Arkansas game we all know and love.

And upstairs Jones Ramsey now said, "Hell, I'd given up, but thank God James Street hasn't."

Although the Longhorns were back in the game, they still needed something else good to happen — and it did. Montgomery brought Arkansas right back, hitting three passes, and the Razorbacks moved 73 yards to the Texas seven-yard line, where it was third down with only 10 minutes left to play. Everybody in both Arkansas and Texas thought the signal to Montgomery from Arkansas' Offensive Coach Don Breaux would be to run the middle and take the field goal. That would make it 17-8, a margin too great for Texas to overcome.

Instead, a pass was ordered, and Montgomery, under a heavy rush, threw short for Dicus, who looked open in the end zone, and up came Danny Lester to intercept. Texas was alive.

Street couldn't move his team immediately but after an exchange of punts, the Longhorns took over at their own 36. Still nothing much worked on the ground, and now it was fourth and three at the 43, less than five minutes to go.

From the sidelines Royal gave Street the play, although he doesn't know why.

"In a case like that, you just suck it up and pick a number," he said. "There's no logic to it. Just a hunch."

It was a bomb, which Street isn't supposed to throw well or complete unless Cotton Speyrer outfights somebody for the ball. But it wasn't Speyrer, just as it wasn't Steve Worster. No Worster-Speyrer sauce. It was a 44-yard spiral to the tight end, Randy Peschel, the only receiver Texas sent out. He went streaking down the sideline, right past the Texas bench, a step ahead of his desperate double coverage. The throw was perfect but Street insisted that Peschel "only made the greatest catch in the history of football."

After "53 Veer Pass," one of the gutsiest calls in the history of football.

The stunning 44-yard play put Texas on Arkansas' 13-yard line. Two plays punched it in. Ted Koy made up for losing two fumbles earlier by crashing 11 yards to the two, then Jim Bertelsen dived across for the touchdown with 3:58 on the clock. Happy Feller's placement provided the winning margin.

> There was still time for a passing team, of course. And Montgomery alarmed the Texas fans by quickly hitting four tosses and moving Arkansas to the Texas 39. But there he floated one out into the flat and Tom Campbell, the son of Texas' defensive coach Mike Campbell, outgrabbed John Rees for it, and the Longhorns were ready to go meet the President.

One of Texas' prizes, if you wanted to call it that, was the privilege of playing Notre Dame in the Cotton Bowl. Under Coach Ara Parseghian, the Irish with an 8-1-1 record agreed to go to their first postseason game since Knute Rockne took the Four Horsemen to the Rose Bowl in 1924.

So it came to pass that on January 1, 1970, the burnt-orange shirted No. 1 Longhorns and the white-shirted, golden-domed No. 5 Irish involved themselves in your classic nail-biter.

It was an affair TCU's Abe Martin would have called "a spellin' bee," and Darrell Royal did call "a knucks-down bloodletting."

The Irish are never without athletes, as just about everybody who speaks the English language is aware of. Even some Romans. This time they came with a team that outweighed Texas 20 pounds per man, and had such talents to avail themselves of as Joe Theismann at quarterback, Tom Gatewood at end, and Mike McCoy in the line.

Both teams played well and traded knockout blows. Then, with less than seven minutes to play, and Notre Dame leading 17 to 14, it was up to James Street to try to take the Longhorns on another winning drive.

What he directed was a 17-play, 76-yard thing of burnt-orange beauty. There was a big 35-yard run by Worster, and twice Street was asked to convert fourth-and-two situations. The last one was unbearably crucial at the Notre Dame 10-yard line. Slick got it with a flat pass that found a leaping Cotton Speyrer at the two.

The Irish made Texas use three plays to score from that close, but Billy Dale took a wishbone handoff from Street and bolted into the end zone behind the blocking of Randy Peschel and Jim Bertelsen, and the Longhorns survived, 21 to 17.

Considering how large the stakes were and how superbly both teams performed, I do believe it was the best bowl game ever played.

And if you'd been with me in the Cotton Bowl that afternoon and had tried to tell me there wouldn't be a Southwest Conference someday, I'm sure I'd have called the white suits to come get you before you hurt yourself.

SIXTEEN

SOME PEOPLE think the Southwest Conference started crumbling in the middle Seventies, even though Texas' Earl Campbell was nabbing spotlights and touchdowns and your Heisman bauble. For one thing, Darrell Royal and Frank Broyles retired — there went a payload of glamor — but something else happened that had an even greater impact. The University of Houston was admitted as a member.

Okay, okay, the Cougars brought a Heisman winner of their own to the dance — Andre Ware in '89 — but I mean, seriously, folks. The Southwest Conference needed the University of Houston about as much as the city of Houston needed more astronauts.

No crowds ever followed the Cougars, and by making them a member the conference intellects eliminated one money-making intersectional game from their own football schedules. A real genius deal. The intellects obviously forgot an age-old fact: football is the straw that stirs the drink.

Some people think the conference started crumbling in 1980 when a little-known cable TV enterprise called ESPN offered a long-range marriage and national exposure, but no money for a while. The conference rejected the offer, saying it wanted money up front.

Those same intellects might ask themselves where ESPN is today in contrast to where the conference is.

Some people think the conference started crumbling in the Eighties when SMU, TCU, Texas A&M, and Houston all went on NCAA probation for recruiting excesses, and everybody else was either investigated by the NCAA, FBI, and CIA, or conducted their own in-house investigations and found — big surprise — "no evidence of any wrongdoing."

Along the way, SMU was even strapped with the "death penalty" for overzealous recruiting habits. SMU fans had enjoyed themselves immensely in the Eighties with all their Pony Expresses, mainly Eric Dickerson, Craig James, and Reggie Dupard, but all of a sudden they were out of football completely for two years, 1987 and 1988.

There were those Southwest Conference observers — count me in — who looked around the country and accused the NCAA of practicing "selective punishment."

Why are you picking on us, we cried, when any fool knows you ought to start the Florida State-Miami game with a burglar alarm?

Which was only one example.

Well, the truth is, the NCAA never wants to catch anybody doing anything wrong — it likes money too much. So what the organization basically did was punish the SWC recruiters for two things:

1. Being sloppy enough to get caught.

2. Being stupid enough to confess.

Some people think the conference started crumbling in the early Nineties when the Arkansas Razorbacks made the mistake of leaving to join the SEC, where they could get consistently beat up by Alabama, Georgia, Florida, Tennessee, LSU, and their other "new friends."

Nevertheless, when Arkansas left the Southwest, there went a lot of packed stadiums, home and away, for the other members.

This in turn sent Texas and Texas A&M looking for survival or greed, whichever came first.

They flirted with the Pac-10, the SEC, and the Big Eight while listening intently to the wisdom of network TV executives, most of whom were too young or too clueless to know who Doak Walker and John David Crow were.

Then some boomer got around to thinking up the idea of Texas and Texas A&M going into the Big Eight, and dragging the unwanted Baylor and Texas Tech along with them, and calling it the Big 12.

So crumbled the SWC for good.

What I'll always wonder is why somebody didn't say to the perpetrators: Hey, you know what? Dallas, Fort Worth and Houston are slightly better TV markets than Waco and Lubbock, or have you been living on Pluto? Instead of doing away with the grand old Southwest Conference, why not dump the Big Eight? Send Nebraska, Oklahoma, Colorado, and Missouri over here, and ask me if I care what happens to Kansas, Iowa State, Kansas State, and Oklahoma State. All of their football histories combined wouldn't make a pimple on the butt of TCU or SMU or Rice.

"Don't get yourself so worked up, old-timer," Billy Clyde said. "Most things happen for the best. Look at it this way...where Arkansas, Baylor, and Texas Tech are now, they'll never win again. But TCU, SMU, and Rice have a chance to recapture the glories of the past."

"Sorry," I said. "I was just trying to be informative."

I'd tried to be informative for Cindy Pritchard, the girl sportswriter from the *Light & Shopper*. She had asked for my thoughts on the sad demise of the Southwest Conference while we watched her get on the outside of a beer and a late dish of chicken and slick dumplings.

She'd been to the TCU pep rally on the campus, where Coach Dennis Franchione had said the Frogs wouldn't be any more intimidated by Southern Cal this time than they'd been in that Sun Bowl in '98 where they scored a 28-to-19 upset over the Trojans.

Then she'd gone downtown to the office to clack out her advance for tomorrow morning's paper.

In a lineup of girl sportswriters, Cindy would win Best in Cute, as Tommy Earl promised. She didn't seem to be eaten up with Title IX either, and claimed she didn't like going into locker rooms any better than I ever had.

She agreed that a men's football or basketball locker room smelled like the armpit of a Greek wrestler — when it didn't smell like an A-rab with a goat under each arm.

I'd already received all the well-wishing long distance calls.

Billy Clyde's Uncle Kenneth called from somewhere on the senior golf tour to say he hoped TCU played dead solid perfect tomorrow.

Juanita Hutchins, the former Fort Worth bartender who turned songwriter, called from Nashville to wish us and TCU luck. I told her things weren't the same without her behind the bar at Herb's Cafe. There weren't near as many discussions about pathos and humor in the Victorian novel.

She said for me to take care of everything in Baja Oklahoma.

Jim Tom Pinch called from Zurich to tell me the game was going to be semi-tough all day long, and I should remind any TCU player I came across that you gotta play hurt.

Billy Clyde's wife, Barbara Jane, and his buddy Shake Tiller called from Hollywood where they were making another movie. Shake commented that big games just seem to keep turning up along the weary road of life its ownself. Barbara Jane said to tell TCU she'd always admired rude behavior in a team. Then she left me with a yell from all of our high school days: "Hey, hey, our team's great ... Let's go, gang ... all the way to State!"

I asked Billy Clyde Puckett, my leading football authority, what he seriously thought about TCU's chances to beat Southern Cal tomorrow.

Grinning, he said, "Oh, I'd say the chances are excellent, wouldn't you? It's your book."

ACKNOWLEDGMENTS

In another time I used to think I only owed thanks to my ribbon reverse, ashtray, and coffee mug. Now it's a lot of people and research material. They call it aging. Anyhow, this particular remembrance couldn't have been undertaken, much less completed, without the help of the following memory jolters:

Here Come the Longhorns, by Lou Maysel; *Football Texas Style,* by Kern Tips; *The Greatest Moments in Southwest Conference History,* by Will Grimsley; *All-America: The Complete Roster of Football's Heroes,* by Bernie McCarty; *About the Cotton Bowl,* by Lee Cruse; *Upon Other Fields on Other Days,* by Jim Koger; *The Fightin' Texas Aggies,* by Gene Schoor; *The Heisman,* by John T. Brady; *Game of the Century,* by J. Neal Blanton; *The Rose Bowl,* by Maxwell Stiles; *Ronald's Encyclopedia of Football,* by Harold Claassen; *The Official 1998 NCAA Football Records Book,* compiled by the NCAA staff; *Centennial '36,* by Kenneth B. Ragsdale; my bound and well-guarded issues of *Illustrated Football Annual* from 1931 through 1951, and my bound and well-guarded issues of *Street and Smith's College Football Yearbook* from 1940 to present.

As for people ...

A courtly bow to Bill Little, the sports information director at the University of Texas. He stood out like a longhorn in the middle of Main Street among those who aided and abetted.

But a hefty thanks to four others of the SID persuasion who always came through when they heard the whimper: Texas A&M's Alan Cannon, SMU's Jon Jackson, Rice's Bill Cousins, and Glen Stone, once of TCU.

Of course, through the years it's been a particular privilege to have gotten to know and even become friends with some of my favorite folklore heroes, such as Darrell Royal, Doak Walker, John David Crow, Davey O'Brien, Sam Baugh, Bear Bryant, Dutch Meyer, Abe Martin, Bobby Layne, Don Meredith, James Street, Dicky Maegle, and Jim Swink, to name only a few. The stuff I learned from them is all through this book.

Finally, a Hollywood-type hug on Dave Burgin, good friend, fan, editor, publisher. It may well have been Dave who thought up this whole deal. I don't know. We were having a junior at the time. I do know he saw that it got done.

— Dan Jenkins

A MAN'S LIFE IN RESEARCH

Here in capital letters are the nation's consensus All-America selections from 1927, the first season in which Southwest Conference players were recognized, through 1995, the final year of the conference.

Southwest Conference players are in bold type. Also included and in boldface are those SWC players along with a few from other Texas colleges who were named to at least one First Team All-America by a reputable authority. As Bear Bryant once said of All-America teams and polls, "If you make one, you can say you made 'em all."

Through the years there have been numerous All-America selectors. The following list reveals those that flourished, some longer than others, throughout the Twenties, Thirties, Forties, and Fifties.

AP, UP, INS, NEA, NANA, *Football Writers*, *Football Coaches*, *The Sporting News*, Grantland Rice (*Collier's*), Bill Stern (*Life*), *The Football News*, Hearst, *Liberty*, *Illustrated Football Annual*, Williamson, *New York Sun*, *New York Journal-American*, *New York World-Telegram*, *New York Mirror*, *New York Daily News*, *Newsweek*, Helms Foundation, Pathe News, Fox Movietone News, Paramount News, *Look*, *Chicago Tribune*, Norman Sper, Eddie Dooley, Jim Crowley, *Mid-Week Pictorial*, *Ohio Journal*, *College Humor*, *Spalding Guide*, *Boston Herald*, *Boston Record*, Kate Smith Radio, Ted Husing Radio, *Kansas City Star*, *Central Press*, All-America Board, East-West Committee, *Houston Post*.

Selectors have decreased drastically over the years, largely — and I might add sadly — because of our daily newspapers choosing to place more emphasis on professional sports. Thus, today's major selectors are generally considered to be the AP, *Football Writers*, *Football Coaches*, Walter Camp Foundation, *The Sporting News*, *The Football News*.

In compiling the list of semi-immortals the author graciously appreciates the aid of two sources — Bernie McCarty's *ALL-AMERICA: The Complete Roster of Football's Heroes*, and the annual *Official NCAA Football Records Book*.

1927

ENDS
BENNIE OOSTERBAAN, Michigan
TOM NASH, Georgia
Rags Matthews, TCU

TACKLES
JESSE HIBBS, USC
BUD SPRAGUE, Army
Loggy Sprott, Texas A&M

GUARDS
BILL WEBSTER, Yale
JOHN P. SMITH, Notre Dame

CENTER
LARRY BETTENCOURT, St. Mary's

BACKS
MORLEY DRURY, USC

CHRIS CAGLE, Army
GIBBY WELCH, Pittsburgh
BRUCE CALDWELL, Yale
HERB JOESTING, Minnesota
BILL SPEARS, VANDERBILT
Joel Hunt, Texas A&M
Gerald Mann, SMU

1928

ENDS
IRV PHILLIPS, California
JOE DONCHESS, Pittsburgh

TACKLES
JESSE HIBBS, USC
OTTO POMMERENING, Michigan
FRANK SPEER, Georgia Tech
Gordy Brown, Texas

GUARDS
SERAPHIM POST, Stanford
RUSS CRANE, Illinois
Choc Sanders, SMU

CENTER
PETER PUND, Georgia Tech

BACKS
CHRIS CAGLE, Army
KEN STRONG, NYU
DUTCH CLARK, Colorado College
HOWARD HARPSTER, Carnegie Tech
CHUCK CARROLL, Washington

1929

ENDS
JOE DONCHESS, Pittsburgh
WES FESLER, Ohio State
Wear Schoonover, Arkansas

TACKLES
BRONKO NAGURSKI, Minnesota
ELMER SLEIGHT, Purdue
Marion (Scrapiron) Hammon, SMU

GUARDS
JACK CANNON, Notre Dame
RAY MONTGOMERY, Pittsburgh
Mike Brumbelow, TCU

CENTER
BEN TICKNOR, Harvard

BACKS
CHRIS CAGLE, Army
FRANK CARIDEO, Notre Dame
RALPH WELCH, Purdue
GENE McEVER, Tennessee
ALBIE BOOTH, Yale

1930

ENDS
WES FESLER, Ohio State
FRANK BAKER, Northwestern

TACKLES
FRED SINGTON, Alabama
MILO LUBRATOVICH, Wisconsin
TURK EDWARDS, Washington State

GUARDS
BARTON (BOCHEY) KOCH, Baylor
TED BECKETT, California

CENTERS
BEN TICKNOR, Harvard
MEL HEIN, Washington State

BACKS
FRANK CARIDEO, Notre Dame

MARCHY SCHWARTZ, Notre Dame
ERMY PINCKERT, USC
LEN MACALUSO, Colgate
BOBBY DODD, Tennessee
Cy Leland, TCU

1931

ENDS
JERRY DALRYMPLE, Tulane
VERNON (CATFISH) SMITH, Georgia

TACKLES
JACK RILEY, Northwestern
JESSE QUATSE, Pittsburgh

GUARDS
JOHNNY BAKER, USC
BIGGIE MUNN, Minnesota
HERMAN HICKMAN, Tennessee

CENTER
TOM YARR, Notre Dame

BACKS
MARCHY SCHWARTZ, Notre Dame
GUS SHAVER, USC
ERNY PINCKERT, USC
BARRY WOOD, Harvard
PUG RENTNER, Northwestern
JOHNNY CAIN, Alabama
Speedy Mason, SMU

1932

ENDS
PAUL MOSS, Purdue
JOE SKLADANY, Pittsburgh

TACKLES
ERNIE SMITH, USC
JOE KURTH, Notre Dame

GUARDS
BILL CORBUS, Stanford
MILT SUMMERFELT, Army
Johnny Vaught, TCU

CENTER
PETE GRACEY, Vanderbilt

BACKS
HARRY NEWMAN, Michigan
WARREN HELLER, Pittsburgh
DON ZIMMERMAN, Tulane
JIMMY HITCHCOCK, Auburn
Harrison Stafford, Texas

1933

ENDS
PAUL GEISLER, Centenary
JOE SKLADANY, Pittsburgh

BUTCH LARSON, Minnesota
Frank James, Baylor
Jim Tom Petty, Baylor

TACKLES
FRANK WISTERT, Michigan
FRED CRAWFORD, Duke
CHARLEY CEPPI, Princeton

GUARDS
BILL CORBUS, Stanford
AARON ROSENBERG, USC

CENTER
CHUCK BERNARD, Michigan

BACKS
COTTON WARBURTON, USC
BEATTIE FEATHERS, Tennessee
DUANE PURVIS, Purdue
GEORGE SAUER, Nebraska
CLIFF MONTGOMERY, Columbia
JACK BUCKLER, Army
Tom Murphy, Arkansas
Joe Jack Pearce, Baylor

1934

ENDS
DON HUTSON, Alabama
BUTCH LARSON, Minnesota

TACKLES
BILL LEE, Alabama
BOB REYNOLDS, Stanford

SLADE CUTTER, Navy
Clyde Carter, SMU

GUARDS
CHUCK HARTWIG, Pittsburgh
BILL BEVAN, Minnesota

CENTER
DARRELL LESTER, TCU

BACKS
DIXIE HOWELL, Alabama
PUG LUND, Minnesota
BUZZ BORRIES, Navy
BOBBY GRAYSON, Stanford
Bill Wallace, Rice
John McCauley, Rice
Bobby Wilson, SMU
Bohn Hilliard, Texas

1935

ENDS
GAYNELL TINSLEY, LSU
MONK MOSCRIP, Stanford
WAYNE MILLNER, Notre Dame

TACKLES
ED WIDSETH, Minnesota
LARRY LUTZ, California
Truman Spain, SMU

GUARDS
J.C. (IRONMAN) WETSEL, SMU
John Weller, Princeton

The 1927 East-West game stars from the SWC: Gerald Mann of SMU, Texas A&M's Joel Hunt and TCU's Rags Matthews.

CENTER
DARRELL LESTER, TCU

BACKS
BOBBY WILSON, SMU
JAY BERWANGER, Chicago
BOBBY GRAYSON, Stanford
RILEY SMITH, Alabama
Sam Baugh, TCU
Harry Shuford, SMU
Bill Wallace, Rice
John McCauley, Rice

1936

ENDS
GAYNELL TINSLEY, LSU
LARRY KELLEY, Yale
Walter Roach, TCU

TACKLES
ED WIDSETH, Minnesota
AV DANIELL, Pittsburgh

GUARDS
STEVE REID, Northwestern
MAX STARCEVICH, Washington
Joe Routt, Texas A&M

CENTERS
ALEX WOJCIECHOWICZ, Fordham
CARL HINKLE, VANDERBILT

BACKS
SAM BAUGH, TCU
ACE PARKER, Duke
BUZZ BUIVID, Marquette
SAM FRANCIS, Nebraska
NELLO FALASCHI, Santa Clara

1937

ENDS
CHUCK SWEENEY, Notre Dame
ANDY BERSHAK, North Carolina
Jim Benton, Arkansas
Sam Boyd, Baylor

TACKLES
ED FRANCO, Fordham
TONY MATISI, Pittsburgh
I.B. Hale, TCU

GUARDS
JOE ROUTT, Texas A&M
LEROY MONSKY, Alabama

CENTERS
ALEX WOJCIECHOWICZ, Fordham
Ki Aldrich, TCU

BACKS
CLINT FRANK, Yale

TCU's first All-America, end Rags Matthews, 1927.

MARSHALL GOLDBERG, Pittsburgh
WHIZZER WHITE, Colorado
SAM CHAPMAN, California
Davey O'Brien, TCU

1938

ENDS
WADDY YOUNG, Oklahoma
BRUD HOLLAND, Cornell
BOWDEN WYATT, Tennessee
Sam Boyd, Baylor

TACKLES
ED BEINOR, Notre Dame
AL WOLFF, Santa Clara
I.B. Hale, TCU

GUARDS
ED BOCK, Iowa State
RALPH HEIKKINEN, Michigan

CENTER
KI ALDRICH, TCU

BACKS
DAVEY O'BRIEN, TCU
MARSHALL GOLDBERG, Pittsburgh
VIC BOTTARI, California
BOB MacLEOD, Dartmouth
SID LUCKMAN, Columbia

Sam pulls the trigger in the Sugar Bowl against LSU.

GEORGE CAFEGO, Tennessee
Billy Patterson, Baylor

1939

ENDS
ESCO SARKKINEN, Ohio State
KEN KAVANAUGH, LSU

TACKLES
JOE BOYD, Texas A&M
NICK DRAHOS, Cornell
HARLEY McCOLLUM, Tulane

GUARDS
HARRY (BLACKJACK) SMITH, USC
BOB SUFFRIDGE, Tennessee
ED MOLINSKI, Tennessee

CENTERS
JOHN SCHIECHL, Santa Clara
Clyde (Bulldog) Turner, Hardin-Simmons

BACKS
JOHN KIMBROUGH, Texas A&M
NILE KINNICK, Iowa
GEORGE CAFEGO, Tennessee
TOM HARMON, Michigan
BANKS McFADDEN, Clemson
GRENNY LANSDELL, USC

1940

ENDS
DAVE RANKIN, Purdue
GENE GOODREAULT, Boston College
PAUL SEVERIN, North Carolina
Jack Russell, Baylor

TACKLES
NICK DRAHOS, Cornell
ALF BAUMAN, Northwestern
URBAN ODSON, Minnesota

GUARDS
MARSHALL ROBNETT, Texas A&M
BOB SUFFRIDGE, Tennessee

CENTERS
RUDY MUCHA, Washington
Bob Nelson, Baylor

BACKS
JOHN KIMBROUGH, Texas A&M
TOM HARMON, Michigan
GEORGE (SONNY) FRANCK, Minnesota
FRANKIE ALBERT, Stanford
CHARLIE O'ROURKE, Boston College
PAUL CHRISTMAN, Missouri
Jack Wilson, Baylor

1941

ENDS
HOLT RAST, Alabama
BOB DOVE, Notre Dame
MAL KUTNER, Texas
Jim Sterling, Texas A&M
Kelly Simpson, SMU
Bill (Jitterbug) Henderson, Texas A&M

TACKLES
DICK WILDUNG, Minnesota
ERNIE BLANDIN, Tulane

GUARDS
CHAL DANIEL, Texas
ENDICOTT PEABODY III, Harvard

CENTER
DAROLD JENKINS, Missouri

BACKS
BRUCE SMITH, Minnesota
FRANK SINKWICH, Georgia
BILL DUDLEY, Virginia
FRANKIE ALBERT, Stanford
BOB WESTFALL, Michigan
Pete Layden, Texas
Derace Moser, Texas A&M
Jack Crain, Texas

1942

ENDS
BOB DOVE, Notre Dame
DAVE SCHREINER, Wisconsin

TACKLES
DICK WILDUNG, Minnesota
AL WISTERT, Michigan
Derrell Palmer, TCU
Stan Maulden, Texas

GUARDS
HARVEY HARDY, Georgia Tech
CHUCK TAYLOR, Stanford
ALEX AGASE, Illinois
Felix Bucek, Texas A&M

CENTER
JOE DOMANOVICH, Alabama

BACKS
FRANK SINKWICH, Georgia
PAUL GOVERNALI, Columbia
BILLY HILLENBRAND, Indiana
MIKE HOLOVAK, Boston College
CLINT CASTLEBERRY, Georgia Tech

1943

ENDS
JOHN YONAKOR, Notre Dame

RALPH HEYWOOD, USC
Joe Parker, Texas

TACKLES
JIM WHITE, Notre Dame
DON WHITMIRE, Navy

GUARDS
PAT FILLEY, Notre Dame
ALEX AGASE, Purdue (Illinois)
Harold Fischer, Southwestern (Texas)
Harry Turley, Texas A&M

CENTERS
CAS MYSLINSKI, Army
Buddy Gatewood, Tulane (Baylor)

BACKS
ANGELO BERTELLI, Notre Dame
BOB ODELL, Penn
CREIGHTON MILLER, Notre Dame
BILL DALEY, Michigan (Minnesota)

1944

ENDS
PHIL TINSLEY, Georgia Tech
PAUL WALKER, Yale
JACK DUGGER, Ohio State
Hub Bechtol, Texas

TACKLES
DON WHITMIRE, Navy
JOHN FERRARO, USC
Clyde Flowers, TCU

GUARDS
BILL HACKETT, Ohio State
BEN CHASE, Navy
H.J. (Ham) Nichols, Rice

CENTERS
JOHN TAVENER, Indiana
Jack Sachse, Texas

BACKS
LES HORVATH, Ohio State
GLENN DAVIS, Army
DOC BLANCHARD, Army
BOB JENKINS, Navy
BOB FENIMORE, Oklahoma A&M

1945

ENDS
HUB BECHTOL, Texas
DICK DUDEN, Navy
BOB RAVENSBURG, Indiana
MAX MORRIS, Northwestern

TACKLES
DEWOTT COULTER, Army
GEORGE SAVITSKY, Penn

The first great SMU backfield, 1935: Bobby Wilson, Johnny Sprague, Shelley Burt and Harry Shuford.

Tom Dean, SMU

GUARDS
WARREN AMLING, Ohio State
JOHN GREEN, Army

CENTER
VAUGHN MANCHA, Alabama

BACKS
GLENN DAVIS, Army
DOC BLANCHARD, Army
BOB FENIMORE, Oklahoma A&M
HERMAN WEDEMEYER, St. Mary's
HARRY GILMER, Alabama

1946

ENDS
HUB BECHTOL, Texas
HANK FOLDBERG, Army
BURR BALDWIN, UCLA

TACKLES
GEORGE CONNOR, Notre Dame
DICK HUFFMAN, Tennessee

GUARDS
WELDON HUMBLE, Rice
ALEX AGASE, Illinois

CENTER
PAUL DUKE, Georgia Tech

BACKS
CHARLEY TRIPPI, Georgia
JOHNNY LUJACK, Notre Dame

GLENN DAVIS, Army
DOC BLANCHARD, Army
ARNOLD TUCKER, Army
Rudy (Doc) Mobley, Hardin-Simmons

1947

ENDS
PAUL CLEARY, USC
BILL SWIACKI, Columbia
BARNEY POOLE, Mississippi

TACKLES
DICK HARRIS, Texas
GEORGE CONNOR, Notre Dame

GUARDS
JOE STEFFY, Army
BILL FISCHER, Notre Dame

CENTER
CHUCK BEDNARIK, Penn

BACKS
DOAK WALKER, SMU
BOBBY LAYNE, Texas
JOHNNY LUJACK, Notre Dame
BOB CHAPPIUS, Michigan
CHARLEY CONERLY, Mississippi

1948

ENDS
DICK RIFENBURG, Michigan
LEON HART, Notre Dame
ART WEINER, North Carolina

TACKLES
AL WISTERT, Michigan
LEO NOMELLINI, Minnesota

GUARDS
BUDDY BURRIS, Oklahoma
BILL FISCHER, Notre Dame

CENTER
CHUCK BEDNARIK, Penn

BACKS
DOAK WALKER, SMU
CLYDE (SMACKOVER) SCOTT, Arkansas
EMIL SITKO, Notre Dame
CHARLEY JUSTICE, North Carolina
JACKIE JENSEN, California

1949

ENDS
JAMES (FROGGY) WILLIAMS, Rice
LEON HART, Notre Dame
JIM OWENS, Oklahoma
J.D. Ison, Baylor

TACKLES
LEO NOMELLINI, Minnesota
AL WISTERT, Michigan
WADE WALKER, Oklahoma

GUARDS
ROD FRANZ, California
ED BAGDON, Michigan State
Bud McFadin, Texas

CENTERS
JOE WATSON, Rice
CLAYTON TONNEMAKER, Minnesota

BACKS
DOAK WALKER, SMU
EMIL SITKO, Notre Dame
ARNOLD GALIFFA, Army
BOB WILLIAMS, Notre Dame
CHARLEY JUSTICE, North Carolina
Lindy Berry, TCU
Adrian Burk, Baylor

1950

ENDS
DAN FOLDBERG, Army
BILL McCOLL, Stanford
FRANK ANDERSON, Oklahoma
Don Menasco, Texas

TACKLES
JIM WEATHERALL, Oklahoma
BOB GAIN, Kentucky

GUARDS
BUD McFADIN, Texas

LES RICHTER, California

CENTER
JERRY GROOM, Notre Dame

BACKS
KYLE ROTE, SMU
VIC JANOWICZ, Ohio State
BABE PARILLI, Kentucky
LEON HEATH, Oklahoma
Bob Smith, Texas A&M

1951

ENDS
BILL HOWTON, Rice
BILL McCOLL, Stanford
BOB CAREY, Michigan State
Stan Williams, Baylor

TACKLES
JIM WEATHERALL, Oklahoma
DON COLEMAN, Michigan State
Doug Conaway, TCU
Jack Little, Texas A&M
Ken Casner, Baylor

GUARDS
BOB WARD, Maryland
LES RICHTER, California
Bill Athey, Baylor

SMU's Kyle
Rote followed
Doak Walker
on a *Life*
cover.

TOP BACK
ON A TOP TEAM
KYLE ROTE

Clyde (Smackover) Scott, Arkansas All-America halfback, 1948

CENTERS
DICK HIGHTOWER, SMU
Keith Flowers, TCU

BACKS
LARRY ISBELL, Baylor
DICK KAZMAIER, Princeton
HANK LAURICELLA, Tennessee
JOHNNY KARRAS, Illinois
BABE PARILLI, Kentucky
Ray McKown, TCU
Bobby Dillon, Texas
1952

ENDS
FRANK McPHEE, Princeton
BERNIE FLOWERS, Purdue
Tom Stolhandske, Texas

TACKLES
DICK MODZELEWSKI, Maryland
HAL MILLER, Georgia Tech
Jack Little, Texas A&M
J.D. Kimmel, Houston

GUARDS
HARLEY SEWELL, Texas
ELMER WILLHOITE, USC
JOHN MICHAELS, Tennessee

CENTERS
DONN MOOMAW, UCLA
Jack Sisco, Baylor

BACKS
BILLY VESSELS, Oklahoma
JOHN LATTNER, Notre Dame
JIM SEARS, USC
JACK SCARBATH, Maryland
LEON HARDEMAN, Georgia Tech
Jerry Coody, Baylor
L.G. (Long Gone) Dupre, Baylor

1953

ENDS
CARLTON MASSEY, Texas
Don Dohoney, Michigan State

TACKLES
STAN JONES, Maryland
ART HUNTER, Notre Dame
James Ray Smith, Baylor
John Hudson, Rice

GUARDS
J.D. ROBERTS, Oklahoma
CRAWFORD MIMS, Mississippi

CENTER
LARRY MORRIS, Georgia Tech

BACKS
KOSSE JOHNSON, Rice
PAUL CAMERON, UCLA
PAUL GIEL, Minnesota
JOHN LATTNER, Notre Dame
J.C. CAROLINE, Illinois

1954

ENDS
MAX BOYDSTUN, Oklahoma
RON BEAGLE, Navy

TACKLES
JACK ELLENA, UCLA
SID FOURNET, LSU
James Ray Smith, Baylor

GUARDS
BUD BROOKS, Arkansas
CALVIN JONES, Iowa

CENTER
KURT BURRIS, Oklahoma

BACKS
DICKY MOEGLE, Rice
HOWARD CASSADY, Ohio State
RALPH GUGLIELMI, Notre Dame
ALAN AMECHE, Wisconsin
BOB DAVENPORT, UCLA

1955

ENDS
RON BEAGLE, Navy
RON KRAMER, Michigan

TACKLES
NORM MASTERS, Michigan State
BRUCE BOSLEY, West Virginia
Herb Gray, Texas

GUARDS
BO BOLINGER, Oklahoma
CALVIN JONES, Iowa
HARDIMAN CURETON, UCLA

CENTERS
BOB PELLEGRINI, Maryland
Hugh Pitts, TCU

BACKS
JIM SWINK, TCU
HOWARD CASSADY, Ohio State
PAUL HORNUNG, Notre Dame
EARL MORRALL, Michigan State

1956

ENDS
RON KRAMER, Michigan
JOE WALTON, Pittsburgh

Rice's King Hill, All-America quarterback, in 1957.

TACKLES
LOU MICHAELS, Kentucky
JOHN WITTE, Oregon State
Norm Hamilton, TCU
Charley Krueger, Texas A&M

GUARDS
BILL GLASS, Baylor
JIM PARKER, Ohio State
Dennis Goehring, Texas A&M

CENTER
JERRY TUBBS, Oklahoma

BACKS
JIM BROWN, Syracuse
TOMMY McDONALD, Oklahoma
JOHNNY MAJORS, Tennessee
JOHN BRODIE, Stanford
PAUL HORNUNG, Notre Dame
Jack Pardee, Texas A&M
Jim Swink, TCU

1957

ENDS
JIMMY PHILLIPS, Auburn
DICK WALLEN, UCLA

TACKLES
CHARLEY KRUEGER, Texas A&M
LOU MICHAELS, Kentucky
ALEX KARRAS, Iowa

GUARDS
BILL KRISHER, Oklahoma
AL ECUYER, Notre Dame

CENTER
DAN CURRIE, Michigan State

BACKS
JOHN DAVID CROW, Texas A&M
KING HILL, Rice
CLENDON THOMAS, Oklahoma
BOB ANDERSON, Army
WALT KOWALCZYK, Michigan State

1958

ENDS
BUDDY DIAL, Rice
SAM WILLIAMS, Michigan State
CURT MERZ, Iowa

TACKLES
DON FLOYD, TCU
BROCK STROM, Air Force
TED BATES, Oregon State
Hogan Wharton, Houston

GUARDS
ZEKE SMITH, Auburn

JOHN GUZIK, Pittsburgh

CENTER
BOB HARRISON, Oklahoma

BACKS
BILLY CANNON, LSU
PETE DAWKINS, Army
RANDY DUNCAN, Iowa
BOB WHITE, Ohio State
Don Meredith, SMU

1959

ENDS
BILL CARPENTER, Army
MONTY STICKLES, Notre Dame

TACKLES
DON FLOYD, TCU
DAN LAMPHEAR, Wisconsin
Bob Lilly, TCU

GUARDS
ROGER DAVIS, Syracuse
BILL BURRELL, Illinois
Maurice Doke, Texas

CENTER
MAXIE BAUGHAN, Georgia Tech

BACKS
BILLY CANNON, LSU
RICHIE LUCAS, Penn State
RON BURTON, Northwestern
CHARLIE FLOWERS, Mississippi
Jack Spikes, TCU
Don Meredith, SMU
Jim Mooty, Arkansas

1960

ENDS
MIKE DITKA, Pittsburgh
DANNY LaROSE, Missouri

TACKLES
BOB LILLY, TCU
KEN RICE, Auburn

GUARDS
TOM BROWN, Minnesota
JOE ROMIG, Colorado

CENTER
E.J. HOLUB, Texas Tech

BACKS
JOE BELLINO, Navy
JAKE GIBBS, Mississippi
ERNIE DAVIS, Syracuse
BOB FERGUSON, Ohio State

Sports Illustrated

DECEMBER 14, 1970   60 CENTS

TEXAS SLAUGHTERS ARKANSAS

Texas' "Woo Woo" Worcester goes long, long.

BOB SCHLOREDT, Washington
Ronnie Bull, Baylor

1961

ENDS
GARY COLLINS, Maryland
BILL MILLER, Miami

TACKLES
BILLY NEIGHBORS, Alabama
MERLIN OLSEN, Utah State
Don Talbert, Texas

GUARDS
ROY WINSTON, LSU
JOE ROMIG, Colorado

CENTER
ALEX KROLL, Rutgers

BACKS
JAMES SAXTON, Texas

ERNIE DAVIS, Syracuse
BOB FERGUSON, Ohio State
SANDY STEPHENS, Minnesota
Lance Alworth, Arkansas
Ronnie Bull, Baylor

1962

ENDS
HAL BEDOLE, USC
PAT RICHTER, Wisconsin

TACKLES
BOBBY BELL, Minnesota
JIM DUNAWAY, Mississippi

GUARDS
JOHNNY TREADWELL, Texas
JACK CVERCKO, Northwestern

CENTER
LEE ROY JORDAN, Alabama

BACKS
TERRY BAKER, Oregon State
JERRY STOVALL, LSU
MEL RENFRO, Oregon
GEORGE SAIMES, Michigan State
Billy Moore, Arkansas

1963

ENDS
LAWRENCE ELKINS, Baylor
VERN BURKE, Oregon State
David Parks, Texas Tech

TACKLES
SCOTT APPLETON, Texas
CARL ELLER, Minnesota

GUARDS
BOB BROWN, Nebraska
RICK REDMAN, Washington

CENTER
DICK BUTKUS, Illinois

BACKS
ROGER STAUBACH, Navy
GALE SAYERS, Kansas
PAUL MARTHA, Pittsburgh
SHERMAN LEWIS, Michigan State
JIM GRISHAM, Oklahoma
Tommy Ford, Texas
Tommy Crutcher, TCU

1964
ENDS
LAWRENCE ELKINS, Baylor
JACK SNOW, Notre Dame
FRED BILETNIKOFF, Florida State

TACKLES
RALPH NEELY, Oklahoma
LARRY KRAMER, Nebraska

GUARDS
TOMMY NOBIS, Texas
RICK REDMAN, Washington
GLENN RESSLER, Penn State
Ronnie Caveness, Arkansas

CENTERS
DICK BUTKUS, Illinois
Malcolm Walker, Rice

BACKS
GALE SAYERS, Kansas
ROGER STAUBACH, Navy
TUCKER FREDERICKSON, Auburn
JOHN HUARTE, Notre Dame
JOE NAMATH, Alabama
Donny Anderson, Texas Tech

1965

OFFENSE
ENDS
HOWARD TWILLEY, Tulsa
FREEMAN WHITE, Nebraska
Bobby Crockett, Arkansas

TACKLES
GLEN RAY HINES, Arkansas
SAM BALL, Kentucky

GUARDS
DICK ARRINGTON, Notre Dame
STAS MALISZEWSKI, Princeton

CENTER
PAUL CRANE, Alabama

BACKS
DONNY ANDERSON, Texas Tech
BOB GRIESE, Purdue
MIKE GARRETT, USC
JIM GRABOWSKI, Illinois

DEFENSE
ENDS
BUBBA SMITH, Michigan State
AARON BROWN, Minnesota

TACKLES
LOYD PHILLIPS, Arkansas
WALT BARNES, Nebraska
BILL YEARBY, Michigan

LINEBACKERS
TOMMY NOBIS, Texas
CARL McADAMS, Oklahoma
FRANK EMANUEL, Tennessee

BACKS
GEORGE WEBSTER, Michigan State
JOHNNY ROLAND, Missouri
NICK RASSAS, Notre Dame

1966

OFFENSE
ENDS
JACK CLANCY, Michigan
RAY PERKINS, Alabama

TACKLES
RON YARY, USC
CECIL DOWDY, Alabama

GUARDS
TOM REGNER, Notre Dame
LaVERNE ALLERS, Nebraska

CENTER
JIM BRELAND, Georgia Tech

BACKS
STEVE SPURRIER, Florida
MEL FARR, UCLA
CLINT JONES, Michigan State
NICK EDDY, Notre Dame

DEFENSE
ENDS
BUBBA SMITH, Michigan State
ALAN PAGE, Notre Dame

TACKLES
LOYD PHILLIPS, Arkansas
TOM GREENLEE, Washington

GUARDS
JOHN LaGRONE, SMU
WAYNE MEYLAN, Nebraska

LINEBACKERS
JIM LYNCH, Notre Dame
PAUL NAUMOFF, Tennessee

BACKS
GEORGE WEBSTER, Michigan State
TOM BEIER, Miami
NATE SHAW, USC

1967

OFFENSE
ENDS
RON SELLERS, Florida State
DENNIS HOMAN, Alabama

TACKLES
RON YARY, USC
ED CHANDLER, Georgia

GUARDS
RICH STOTTER, Houston
HARRY OLSZEWSKI, Clemson

CENTER
BOB JOHNSON, Tennessee

BACKS
GARY BEBAN, UCLA
O.J. SIMPSON, USC
LEROY KEYES, Purdue
LARRY CSONKA, Syracuse

DEFENSE
ENDS
TED HENDRICKS, Miami
TIM ROSSOVICH, USC

TACKLES
DENNIS BYRD, North Carolina State
GREG PIPES, Baylor

GUARDS
GRANVILLE LIGGINS, Oklahoma
WAYNE MEYLAN, Nebraska

LINEBACKERS
ADRIAN YOUNG, USC
DON MANNING, UCLA
Corby Robertson, Texas
Billy Hobbs, Texas A&M

BACKS
DICK ANDERSON, Colorado
BOBBY JOHNS, Alabama
TOM SCHOEN, Notre Dame
FRANK LORIA, Virginia Tech

1968

OFFENSE
ENDS
JERRY LEVIAS, SMU
TED KWALICK, Penn State

TACKLES
DAVE FOLEY, Ohio State
GEORGE KUNZ, Notre Dame

GUARDS
JIM BARNES, Arkansas
MIKE MONTLER, Colorado

CENTER
JOHN DIDION, Oregon State

BACKS
CHRIS GILBERT, Texas
O.J. SIMPSON, USC
LEROY KEYES, Purdue
TERRY HANRATTY, Notre Dame

DEFENSE
ENDS
TED HENDRICKS, Miami
JOHN ZOOK, Kansas

TACKLES
JOE GREENE, North Texas State
BILL STANFILL, Georgia
Loyd Wainscott, Texas
Rolf Krueger, Texas A&M

GUARDS
CHUCK KYLE, Purdue
ED WHITE, California

LINEBACKERS
STEVE KINER, Tennessee
DENNIS ONKOTZ, Penn State
Billy Hobbs, Texas A&M

BACKS
JAKE SCOTT, Georgia
ROGER WEHRLI, Missouri
AL WORLEY, Washington
Tommy Maxwell, Texas A&M

1969

OFFENSE
ENDS
JIM MANDICH, Michigan
CARLOS ALVAREZ, Florida
WALKER GILLETTE, Richmond
Cotton Speyrer, Texas
Chuck Dicus, Arkansas
Richard Campbell, Texas Tech

TACKLES
BOB McKAY, Texas
JOHN WARD, Oklahoma
Bobby Wuensch, Texas

GUARDS
BILL BRIDGES, Houston
CHIP KELL, Tennessee

CENTER
RODNEY BRAND, Arkansas

BACKS
STEVE WORSTER, Texas
MIKE PHIPPS, Purdue
STEVE OWENS, Oklahoma
JIM OTIS, Ohio State

DEFENSE
ENDS
JIM GUNN, USC
PHIL OLSEN, Utah State

TACKLES
MIKE REID, Penn State
MIKE McCOY, Notre Dame

MIDDLE GUARD
JIM STILLWAGON, Ohio State

LINEBACKERS
STEVE KINER, Tennessee
DENNIS ONKOTZ, Penn State
MIKE BALLOU, UCLA
Glen Halsell, Texas
Cliff Powell, Arkansas

BACKS
JACK TATUM, Ohio State
TOM CURTIS, Michigan
BUDDY McCLINTON, Auburn
Denton Fox, Texas Tech

1970

OFFENSE
ENDS
ELMO WRIGHT, Houston
TOM GATEWOOD, Notre Dame
ERNIE JENNINGS, Air Force
Cotton Speyrer, Texas
Chuck Dicus, Arkansas

TACKLES
BOBBY WUENSCH, Texas
DON DIERDORT, Michigan

GUARDS
CHIP KELL, Tennessee
LARRY DiNARDO, Notre Dame

CENTER
DON POPPLEWELL, Colorado

BACKS
STEVE WORSTER, Texas
JIM PLUNKETT, Stanford
DON McCAULEY, North Carolina
TOMMY CASANOVA, LSU

DEFENSE
ENDS
BILL ATESSIS, Texas
CHARLIE WEAVER, USC
Bruce James, Arkansas

TACKLES
DICK BUMPAS, Arkansas
ROCK PERDONI, Georgia Tech

MIDDLE GUARD
JIM STILLWAGON, Ohio State

LINEBACKERS
JACK HAM, Penn State
MIKE ANDERSON, LSU

BACKS
DAVE ELMENDORF, Texas A&M
JACK TATUM, Ohio State

LARRY WILLINGHAM, Auburn

1971

OFFENSE
ENDS
JOHNNY RODGERS, Nebraska
TERRY BEASLEY, Auburn

TACKLES
JERRY SISEMORE, Texas
DAVE JOYNER, Penn State

GUARDS
REGGIE McKENZIE, Michigan
ROYCE SMITH, Georgia

CENTER
TOM BRAHANEY, Oklahoma

BACKS
PAT SULLIVAN, Auburn
GREG PRUIT, Oklahoma
ED MARINARO, Cornell
JOHNNY MUSSO, Alabama

DEFENSE
ENDS
WILLIE HARPER, Nebraska
WALT PATULSKI, Notre Dame

TACKLES
LARRY JACOBSON, Nebraska
SHERMAN WHITE, California
MEL LONG, Toledo
RICH GLOVER, Nebraska

LINEBACKERS
MIKE TAYLOR, Michigan
JEFF SIEMON, Stanford

BACKS
TOMMY CASANOVA, LSU
CLARENCE ELLIS, Notre Dame
BOBBY MAJORS, Tennessee

1972

OFFENSE
ENDS
JOHNNY RODGERS, Nebraska
CHARLES YOUNG, USC

TACKLES
JERRY SISEMORE, Texas
PAUL SEYMOUR, Michigan

GUARDS
JOHN HANNAH, Alabama
RON RUSNAK, North Carolina

CENTER
TOM BRAHANEY, Oklahoma

BACKS
BERT JONES, LSU
GREG PRUIT, Oklahoma
OTIS ARMSTRONG, Purdue
WOODY GREEN, Arizona State
Roosevelt Leaks, Texas

DEFENSE

ENDS
ROGER GOREE, Baylor
WILLIE HARPER, Nebraska
BRUCE BANNON, Penn State

TACKLES
GREG MARX, Notre Dame
DAVE BUTZ, Purdue

MIDDLE GUARD
RICH GLOVER, Nebraska

LINEBACKERS
RANDY GRADISHAR, Ohio State
JOHN SKORUPAN, Penn State
Randy Braband, Texas

BACKS
ROBERT POPELKA, SMU
CULLEN BRYANT, Colorado
BRAD VAN PELT, Michigan State
RANDY LOGAN, Michigan

1973

OFFENSE
ENDS
LYNN SWANN, USC
DAVE CASPER, Notre Dame

TACKLES
JOHN HICKS, Ohio State
BOOKER BROWN, USC

GUARDS
BUDDY BROWN, Alabama
BILL YOEST, North Carolina State

CENTER
BILL WYMAN, Texas

BACKS
ROOSEVELT LEAKS, Texas
DAVE JAYNES, Kansas
WOODY GREEN, Arizona State
KERMIT JOHNSON, UCLA
JOHN CAPPELLETTI, Penn State
Dicky Morton, Arkansas

1974

OFFENSE
ENDS
PETE DEMMERLE, Notre Dame
BENNY CUNNINGHAM, Clemson

Oscar Roan, SMU
TACKLES
KURT SCHUMACHER, Ohio State
MARV CRENSHAW, Nebraska

GUARDS
KEN HUFF, North Carolina
JOHN ROUSH, Oklahoma

CENTERS
STEVE MYERS, Ohio State
Aubrey Schulz, Baylor

BACKS
ARCHIE GRIFFIN, Ohio State
JOE WASHINGTON, Oklahoma
ANTHONY DAVIS, USC
STEVE BARTKOWSKI, California

DEFENSE
LINEMEN
RANDY WHITE, Maryland
LEROY COOK, Alabama
PAT DONOVAN, Stanford
MIKE HARTENSTINE, Penn State
Doug English, Texas

MIDDLE GUARD
LOUIE KELCHER, SMU

LINEBACKERS
ROD SHOATE, Oklahoma
RICHARD WOOD, USC
WOODROW LOW, Alabama
Derrell Luce, Baylor

BACKS
PAT THOMAS, Texas A&M
DAVE BROWN, Michigan
JOHN PROVOST, Holy Cross

1975

OFFENSE
ENDS
STEVE RIVERA, California
LARRY SEIVERS, Tennessee

TACKLES
BOB SIMMONS, Texas
DENNIS LICK, Wisconsin
Mike Hughes, Baylor

GUARDS
RANDY JOHNSON, Georgia
TED SMITH, Ohio State

CENTER
RIK BONNESS, Nebraska

BACKS
ARCHIE GRIFFIN, Ohio State
RICKY BELL, USC

JOHN SCIARRA, UCLA
CHUCK MUNCIE, California
Earl Campbell, Texas
Marty Akins, Texas

DEFENSE
ENDS
JIMBO ELROD, Oklahoma
LEROY COOK, Alabama

TACKLES
LEE ROY SELMON, Oklahoma
STEVE NIEHAUS, Notre Dame

MIDDLE GUARD
DEWEY SELMON, Oklahoma

LINEBACKERS
ED SIMONINI, Texas A&M
GREG BUTTLE, Penn State
SAMMY GREEN, Florida
Garth Ten Napel, Texas A&M

BACKS
PAT THOMAS, Texas A&M
TIM FOX, Ohio State
CHET MOELLER, Navy

1976

OFFENSE
ENDS
LARRY SEIVERS, Tennessee
KEN MacAFEE, Notre Dame

TACKLES
CHRIS WARD, Ohio State
MIKE VAUGHAN, Oklahoma

GUARDS
JOEL PARRISH, Georgia
MARK DONAHUE, Michigan

CENTER
DERREL GOFOURTH, Oklahoma State

SMU's "Pony Express," Eric Dickerson and Craig James.

BACKS
TOMMY KRAMER, Rice
TONY DORSETT, Pittsburgh
RICKY BELL, USC
ROB LYTLE, Michigan

DEFENSE
ENDS
ROSS BROWNER, Notre Dame
BOB BRUDZINSKI, Ohio State

TACKLES
WILSON WHITLEY, Houston
GARY JETER, USC

MIDDLE GUARD
AL ROMANO, Pittsburgh

LINEBACKERS
ROBERT JACKSON, Texas A&M
JERRY ROBINSON, UCLA
Thomas Howard, Texas Tech

BACKS
GARY GREEN, Baylor
DENNIS THURMAN, USC
BILL ARMSTRONG, Wake Forest

KICKERS
TONY FRANKLIN, Texas A&M
RUSSELL ERXLEBEN, Texas
STEVE LITTLE, Arkansas

1977

OFFENSE
ENDS
JOHN JEFFERSON, Arizona State
OZZIE NEWSOME, Alabama

TACKLES
DAN IRONS, Texas Tech
CHRIS WARD, Ohio State

GUARDS
LEOTIS HARRIS, Arkansas
MARK DONAHUE, Michigan

CENTER
TOM BRZOZA, Pittsburgh

BACKS
EARL CAMPBELL, Texas
TERRY MILLER, Oklahoma State
CHARLES ALEXANDER, LSU
GUY BENJAMIN, Stanford
Ben Cowins, Arkansas

DEFENSE
LINEMEN
BRAD SHEARER, Texas
ROSS BROWNER, Notre Dame

ART STILL, Kentucky
RANDY HOLLOWAY, Pittsburgh
DEE HARDISON, North Carolina

LINEBACKERS
JERRY ROBINSON, UCLA
TOM COUSINEAU, Ohio State
GARY SPANI, Kansas State

BACKS
DENNIS THURMAN, USC
ZAC HENDERSON, Oklahoma
LUTHER BRADLEY, Notre Dame
BOB JURY, Pittsburgh

KICKERS
RUSSELL ERXLEBEN, Texas
STEVE LITTLE, Arkansas

1978

OFFENSE
ENDS
EMANUEL TOLBERT, SMU
KELLEN WINSLOW, Missouri
Johnny (Lam) Jones, Texas

TACKLES
KELVIN CLARK, Nebraska
KEITH DORNEY, Penn State

GUARDS
GREG ROBERTS, Oklahoma
PAT HOWELL, USC

CENTER
DAVE HUFFMAN, Notre Dame

BACKS
BILLY SIMS, Oklahoma
CHARLES WHITE, USC
CHUCK FUSINA, Penn State
TED BROWN, North Carolina State
CHARLES ALEXANDER, LSU
Ben Cowins, Arkansas

DEFENSE
LINEMEN
MARTY LYONS, Alabama
BRUCE CLARK, Penn State
HUGH GREEN, Pittsburgh
AL HARRIS, Arizona State
MIKE BELL, Colorado State
Jimmy Walker, Arkansas
Steve McMichael, Texas

LINEBACKERS
BOB GOLIC, Notre Dame
JERRY ROBINSON, UCLA
TOM COUSINEAU, Ohio State
Mike Singletary, Baylor

BACKS
JOHNNIE JOHNSON, Texas
KEN EASLEY, UCLA
JEFF NIXON, Richmond

KICKERS
TONY FRANKLIN, Texas A&M
RUSSELL ERXLEBEN, Texas

1979

OFFENSE
ENDS
JOHNNY (LAM) JONES, Texas
KEN MARGERUM, Stanford
JUNIOR MILLER, Nebraska

TACKLES
GREG KOLENDA, Arkansas
JIM BUNCH, Alabama
Melvin Jones, Houston

GUARDS
BRAD BUDDE, USC
KEN FRITZ, Ohio State

CENTER
JIM RITCHER, North Carolina State

BACKS
MARC WILSON, Brigham Young
CHARLES WHITE, USC
BILLY SIMS, Oklahoma
VAGAS FERGUSON, Notre Dame

DEFENSE
LINEMEN
STEVE McMICHAEL, Texas
HUGH GREEN, Pittsburgh
BRUCE CLARK, Penn State
JIM STUCKEY, Clemson
RON SIMMONS, Florida
Jacob Green, Texas A&M

LINEBACKERS
MIKE SINGLETARY, Baylor
GEORGE CUMBY, Oklahoma
RIB SIMPKINS, Michigan

BACKS
JOHNNIE JOHNSON, Texas
KEN EASLEY, UCLA
ROLAND JAMES, Tennessee

1980

OFFENSE
RECEIVERS
KEN MARGERUM, Stanford
DAVE YOUNG, Purdue

LINEMEN
MARK MAY, Pittsburgh

KEITH VAN HORNE, USC
LOUIS OUBRE, Oklahoma
NICK EYRE, Brigham Young
RANDY SCHLEUSENER, Nebraska
Frank Ditta, Baylor

CENTER
JOHN SCULLY, Notre Dame

BACKS
MARK HERMANN, Purdue
HERSCHEL WALKER, Georgia
GEORGE ROGERS, South Carolina
JARVIS REDWINE, Nebraska

DEFENSE
LINEMEN
KENNETH SIMS, Texas
LEONARD MITCHELL, Houston
HUGH GREEN, Pittsburgh
E.J. JUNIOR, Alabama
RON SIMMONS, Florida

LINEBACKERS
MIKE SINGLETARY, Baylor
BOB CRABLE, Notre Dame
LAWRENCE TAYLOR, North Carolina
DAVID LITTLE, Florida

BACKS
JOHN SIMMONS, SMU
RONNIE LOTT, USC
KEN EASLEY, UCLA

1981

OFFENSE
RECEIVERS
STANLEY WASHINGTON, TCU
ANTHONY CARTER, Michigan
TIM WRIGHTMAN, UCLA

LINEMEN
TERRY TAUSCH, Texas
ROY FOSTER, USC
SEAN FARRELL, Penn State
TERRY CROUCH, Oklahoma

CENTER
DAVE RIMINGTON, Nebraska

BACKS
JIM McMAHON, Brigham Young
HERSCHEL WALKER, Georgia
MARCUS ALLEN, USC
HOMER JORDAN, Clemson

DEFENSE
LINEMEN
KENNETH SIMS, Texas
BILLY RAY SMITH, Arkansas
HARVEY ARMSTRONG, SMU

ANDRE TIPPETT, Iowa
TIM KRUMRIE, Wisconsin

LINEBACKERS
BOB CRABLE, Notre Dame
JEFF DAVIS, Clemson
SAL SUNSERI, Pittsburgh

BACKS
TERRY KINARD, Clemson
TOMMY WILCOX, Alabama
FRED MARION, Miami
REG ROBY, Iowa

1982

OFFENSE
RECEIVERS
ANTHONY CARTER, Michigan
GORDON HUDSON, Brigham Young

LINEMEN
STEVE KORTE, Arkansas
JIMBO COVERT, Pittsburgh
DON MOSEBAR, USC
BRUCE MATTHEWS, USC

CENTER
DAVE RIMINGTON, Nebraska

BACKS
ERIC DICKERSON, SMU
JOHN ELWAY, Stanford
HERSCHEL WALKER, Georgia
MIKE ROZIER, Nebraska
Craig James, SMU

DEFENSE
LINEMEN
BILLY RAY SMITH, Arkansas
GABRIEL RIVERA, Texas Tech
WILBER MARSHALL, Florida
VERNON MAXWELL, Arizona State
RICK BRYAN, Oklahoma
MIKE PITTS, Alabama
GEORGE ACHICA, USC

LINEBACKERS
DARRYL TALLEY, West Virginia
RICKY HUNLEY, Arizona
MARCUS MAREK, Ohio State

BACKS
TERRY KINARD, Clemson
TERRY HOAGE, Georgia
MIKE RICHARDSON, Arizona State

1983

OFFENSE
RECEIVERS
IRVING FRYAR, Nebraska

GORDON HUDSON, Brigham Young
Gerald McNeil, Baylor

LINEMEN
DOUG DAWSON, Texas
BILL FRALIC, Pittsburgh
DEAN STEINKUHLER, Nebraska
TERRY LONG, East Carolina

CENTER
TONY SLATON, USC

BACKS
STEVE YOUNG, Brigham Young
MIKE ROZIER, Nebraska
BO JACKSON, Auburn
GREG ALLEN, Florida State
NAPOLEON McCALLUM, Navy

DEFENSE
LINEMEN
REGGIE WHITE, Tennessee
WILLIAM (REFRIGERATOR) PERRY, Clemson
RICK BRYAN, Oklahoma
WILLIAM FULLER, North Carolina

LINEBACKERS
JEFF LEIDING, Texas
WILBER MARSHALL, Florida
RICKY HUNLEY, Arizona
ROB RIVERA, California

BACKS
RUSSELL CARTER, SMU
JERRY GRAY, Texas
TERRY HOAGE, Georgia
DON ROGERS, UCLA
Mossy Cade, Texas

1984

OFFENSE
RECEIVERS
DAVID WILLIAMS, Illinois
EDDIE BROWN, Miami
JAY NOVACEK, Wyoming

LINEMEN
BILL FRALIC, Pittsburgh
LOMAS BROWN, Florida
DEL WILKES, South Carolina
JIM LACHEY, Ohio State
BILL MAYO, Tennessee

CENTER
MARK TRAYNOWICZ, Nebraska

BACKS
KENNETH DAVIS, TCU
DOUG FLUTIE, Boston College
REUBEN MAYES, Washington
KEITH BYARS, Ohio State

DEFENSE
LINEMEN
TONY DEGRATE, Texas
BRUCE SMITH, Virginia Tech
TONY CASILLAS, Oklahoma
RON HOLMES, Washington
Ray Childress, Texas A&M

LINEBACKERS
JACK DEL RIO, USC
GREGG CARR, Auburn
LARRY STATION, Iowa

BACKS
JERRY GRAY, Texas
TONY THURMAN, Boston College
JEFF SANCHEZ, Georgia
ROD BROWN, Oklahoma State
DAVID FULCHER, Arizona State

1985

OFFENSE
RECEIVERS
DAVID WILLIAMS, Illinois
TIM McGEE, Tennessee
WILLIE SMITH, Miami

LINEMEN
JIM DOMBROWSKI, Virginia
JEFF BREGEL, USC
BRIAN JOZWIAK, West Virginia
JOHN RIENSTRA, Temple
JAMIE DUKES, Florida State
J.D. MAARLEVELD, Maryland
Doug Williams, Texas A&M

CENTER
PETE ANDERSON, Georgia

BACKS
REGGIE DUPARD, SMU
CHUCK LONG, Iowa
BO JACKSON, Auburn
THURMAN THOMAS, Oklahoma State
NAPOLEON McCALLUM, Navy
LORENZO WHITE, Michigan State

DEFENSE
LINEMEN
TONY CASILLAS, Oklahoma
TIM GREEN, Syracuse
LES O'NEAL, Oklahoma State
MIKE RUTH, Boston College
MIKE HAMMERSTEIN, Michigan

LINEBACKERS
JOHNNY HOLLAND, Texas A&M
BRIAN BOSWORTH, Oklahoma
LARRY STATION, Iowa

BACKS
DAVID FULCHER, Arizona State

BRAD COCHRAN, Michigan
SCOTT THOMAS, Air Force
BARRY HELTON, Colorado
Thomas Everett, Baylor

1986

OFFENSE
RECEIVERS
CHRIS CARTER, Ohio State
KEITH JACKSON, Oklahoma

LINEMEN
JEFF BREGEL, USC
RANDY DIXON, Pittsburgh
DANNY VILLA, Arizona State
JOHN CLAY, Missouri

CENTER
BEN TAMBURELLO, Auburn

BACKS
VINNY TESTAVERDE, Miami
D. J. DOZIER, Penn State
BRENT FULLWOOD, Auburn
PAUL PALMER, Temple
TERRY FLAGLER, Clemson
BRAD MUSTER, Stanford

DEFENSE
LINEMEN
JEROME BROWN, Miami
DANNY NOONAN, Nebraska
JASON BUCK, Brigham Young
TONY WOODS, Pittsburgh
REGGIE ROGERS, Washington

LINEBACKERS
BRIAN BOSWORTH, Oklahoma
CORNELIUS BENNETT, Alabama
SHANE CONLAN, Penn State
CHRIS SPIELMAN, Ohio State
Johnny Holland, Texas A&M

BACKS
THOMAS EVERETT, Baylor
BENNIE BLADES, Miami
ROD WOODSON, Purdue
GARLAND RIVERS, Michigan
TIM McDONALD, USC

1987

OFFENSE
RECEIVERS
TIM BROWN, Notre Dame
WENDELL DAVIS, LSU
KEITH JACKSON, Oklahoma
Jason Phillips, Houston

LINEMEN
JOHN ELLIOTT, Michigan
MARK HUTSON, Oklahoma

DAVE CADIGAN, USC
RANDY McDANIEL, Arizona State

CENTER
NACHO ALBERGAMO, LSU

BACKS
DON McPHERSON, Syracuse
LORENZO WHITE, Michigan State
CRAIG HEYWOOD, Pittsburgh
TODD SANTOS, San Diego State

DEFENSE
LINEMEN
JOHN ROPER, Texas A&M
DANIEL STUBBS, Miami
CHAD HENNINGS, Air Force
TRACY ROCKER, Auburn
TED GREGORY, Syracuse
Tony Cherico, Arkansas

LINEBACKERS
CHRIS SPIELMAN, Ohio State
DANTE JONES, Oklahoma
AUNDRAY BRUCE, Auburn

BACKS
DEION SANDERS, Florida State
BENNIE BLADES, Miami
RICKEY DIXON, Oklahoma
CHUCK CECIL, Arizona

1988

OFFENSE
RECEIVERS
JASON PHILLIPS, Houston
HART LEE DYKES, Oklahoma State
MARV COOK, Iowa

LINEMEN
ANTHONY PHILLIPS, Oklahoma
TONY MANDARICH, Michigan
MIKE UTLEY, Washington State
MARK STEPNOSKI, Pittsburgh

CENTERS
JAKE YOUNG, Nebraska
JOHN VITALE, Michigan

BACKS
TROY AIKMAN, UCLA
STEVE WALSH, Miami
BARRY SANDERS, Oklahoma State
TIM WORLEY, Georgia
ANTHONY THOMPSON, Indiana
Darren Lewis, Texas A&M

DEFENSE
LINEMEN
WAYNE MARTIN, Arkansas
FRANK STAMS, Notre Dame
TRACY ROCKER, Auburn

MARK MESSNER, Michigan
BILL HAWKINS, Miami

LINEBACKERS
DERRICK THOMAS, Alabama
BRODERICK THOMAS, Nebraska
MIKE STONEBREAKER, Notre Dame
Britt Hager, Texas

BACKS
DEION SANDERS, Florida State
LOUIS OLIVER, Florida
DONNELL WOODFORD, Clemson
DARRYL HENLEY, UCLA

KICKER
KENDALL TRAINOR, Arkansas

1989

OFFENSE
RECEIVERS
MANNY HAZARD, Houston
CLARKSTON HINES, Duke
TERRY MATHIS, New Mexico
MIKE BUSCH, Iowa State

LINEMEN
JIM MABRY, Arkansas
BOB KULA, Michigan State
MOHAMMED ELEWONIBI, Brigham Young
JOE GARTEN, Colorado
ERIC STILL, Tennessee

CENTER
JAKE YOUNG, Nebraska

BACKS
ANDRE WARE, Houston
EMMITT SMITH, Florida
ANTHONY THOMPSON, Indiana
James Gray, Texas Tech

DEFENSE
LINEMEN
GREG MARK, Miami
CHRIS ZORICH, Notre Dame
TIM RYAN, USC
MOE GARDNER, Illinois

LINEBACKERS
JAMES FRANCIS, Baylor
PERCY SNOW, Michigan State
KEITH McCANTS, Alabama
ALFRED WILLIAMS, Colorado

BACKS
TODD LYGHT, Notre Dame
TRIPP WELBORNE, Michigan
LEROY BUTLER, Florida State
MARK CARRIER, USC

1990

OFFENSE
RECEIVERS
ROCKET ISMAIL, Notre Dame
HERMAN MOORE, Virginia
CHRIS SMITH, Brigham Young
Manny Hazard, Houston

LINEMEN
ANTONE DAVIS, Tennessee
JOE GARTEN, Colorado
ED KING, Auburn
STACY LONG, Clemson

CENTERS
JOHN FLANNERY, Syracuse
Mike Arthur, Texas A&M

BACKS
DARREN LEWIS, Texas A&M
TY DETMER, Brigham Young
ERIC BIENIEMY, Colorado
GLYN MILBURN, Stanford

DEFENSE
LINEMEN
RUSSELL MARYLAND, Miami
CHRIS ZORICH, Notre Dame
MOE GARDNER, Illinois
DAVID ROCKER, Auburn

LINEBACKERS
MAURICE CRUM, Miami
MIKE STONEBREAKER, Notre Dame
AFRED WILLIAMS, Colorado

BACKS
TRIPP WELBORNE, Michigan
KEN SWILLING, Georgia Tech
TODD LYGHT, Notre Dame
DARRYLL LEWIS, Arizona
Stanley Richard, Texas

1991

OFFENSE
RECEIVERS
KELLY BLACKWELL, TCU
DESMOND HOWARD, Michigan
MARIO BAILEY, Washington

LINEMEN
GREG SKREPENAK, Michigan
BOB WHITFIELD, Stanford
JEB FLESCH, Clemson
JERRY OSTROSKI, Tulsa
MIRKO JURKOVIC, Notre Dame

CENTER
JAY LEEUWENBRUG, Colorado

BACKS
TREVOR COBB, Rice
TY DETMER, Brigham Young
RUSSELL WHITE, California
VAUGHN DUNBAR, Indiana

DEFENSE
LINEMEN
SANTANA DOTSON, Baylor
STEVE EMTMAN, Washington
BRAD CULPEPPER, Florida
LEROY SMITH, Iowa
Shane Dronett, Texas

LINEBACKERS
MARVIN JONES, Florida State
LEVON KIRKLAND, Clemson
ROBERT JONES, East Carolina

BACKS
KEVIN SMITH, Texas A&M
TERRELL BUCKLEY, Florida State
DALE CARTER, Tennessee
DARRYL WILLIAMS, Miami

KICKER
MARK BOUNDS, Texas Tech

1992

OFFENSE
RECEIVERS
O.J. McDUFFIE, Penn State
SEAN DAWKINS, California
CHRIS GEDNEY, Syracuse
Lloyd Hill, Texas Tech

LINEMEN
AARON TAYLOR, Notre Dame
LINCOLN KENNEDY, Washington
WILLIE ROAF, Louisiana Tech
EV LINDSEY, Mississippi
WILL SHIELDS, Nebraska

CENTER
MIKE COMPTON, West Virginia

BACKS
TREVOR COBB, Rice
GINO TORRETTA, Miami
MARSHALL FAULK, San Diego State
GARRISON HEARST, Georgia

DEFENSE
LINEMEN
ERIC CURRY, Alabama
JOHN COPELAND, Alabama
CHRIS SLADE, Virginia
ROB WALDROP, Arizona

LINEBACKERS
MARCUS BUCKLEY, Texas A&M
MARVIN JONES, Florida State

MIKE BARROW, Miami

BACKS
CARLTON McDONALD, Air Force
CARLTON GRAY, UCLA
DEAN FIGURES, Colorado
RYAN McNEIL, Miami
Patrick Bates, Texas A&M
Lance Gunn, Texas

1993

OFFENSE
RECEIVERS
J. J. STOKES, UCLA
JOHNNIE MORTON, USC
CHRIS PENN, Tulsa

LINEMEN
AARON TAYLOR, Notre Dame
MARK DIXON, Virginia
STACY SEEGARS, Clemson
WAYNE GANDY, Auburn

CENTER
JIM PYNE, Virginia Tech

BACKS
CHARLIE WARD, Florida State
MARSHALL FAULK, San Diego State
LESHON JOHNSON, Northern Illinois
DAVID PALMER, Alabama

DEFENSE
LINEMEN
SAM ADAMS, Texas A&M
ROB WALDROP, Arizona
DAN WILKINSON, Ohio State

LINEBACKERS
TREV ALBERTS, Nebraska
DERRICK BROOKS, Florida State
JAMIR MILLER, UCLA

BACKS
AARON GLENN, Texas A&M
ANTONIO LANGHAM, Alabama
JEFF BURRIS, Notre Dame
COREY SAWYER, Florida State

1994

OFFENSE
RECEIVERS
JACK JACKSON, Florida
MIKE WESTBROOK, Colorado
PETE MITCHELL, Boston College

LINEMEN
TONY BOSELLI, USC
ZACH WIEGERT, Nebraska
KOREY STRINGER, Ohio State
BRENDEN STAI, Nebraska

Blake Brockermeyer, Texas

CENTER
CORY RAYMER, Wisconsin

BACKS
LEELAND McELROY, Texas A&M
KERRY COLLINS, Penn State
KI-JANA CARTER, Penn State
RASHAAM SALAAM, Colorado

DEFENSE
LINEMEN
WARREN SAPP, Miami
KEVIN CARTER, Florida
LUTHER ELLISS, Utah
TEDY BRUSCHI, Arizona

LINEBACKERS
DERRICK BROOKS, Florida State
DANA HOWARD, Illinois
ED STEWART, Nebraska
Antonio Armstrong, Texas A&M
Zach Thomas, Texas Tech

BACKS
CLIFTON ABRAHAM, Florida State
BOBBY TAYLOR, Notre Dame
CHRIS HUDSON, Colorado
TONY BOUIE, Arizona

1995

OFFENSE
RECEIVERS
KEYSHAWN JOHNSON, USC
TERRY GLENN, Ohio State
MARCO BATTAGLIA, Rutgers
Pat Fitzgerald, Texas

LINEMEN
ORLANDO PACE, Ohio State
JEFF HARTINGS, Penn State
JONATHON OGDEN, UCLA
JASON ODOM, Florida
Dan Neil, Texas

CENTER
CLAY SHIVER, Florida State

BACKS
LEELAND McELROY, Texas A&M
TOMMIE FRAZIER, Nebraska
EDDIE GEORGE, Ohio State
TROY DAVIS, Iowa State

DEFENSE
LINEMEN
TONY BRACKENS, Texas
MARCUS JONES, North Carolina
CORNELL BROWN, Virginia Tech
TEDY BRUSCHI, Arizona
Brandon Mitchell, Texas A&M

LINEBACKERS
ZACH THOMAS, Texas Tech
KEVIN HARDY, Illinois

BACKS
RAY MICKENS, Texas A&M
AARON BEASLEY, West Virginia
LAWYER MILLOY, Washington

CHRIS CANTY, Kansas State
GREG MYERS, Colorado State
Marcus Coleman, Texas Tech
Winkie Robinson, Baylor

KICKER
MICHAEL REEDER, TCU

The All-Decade Teams of the Southwest
(Selected entirely by me and my research)

1900-1919

ENDS
Maxey Hart, Texas
Shirley Brick, Rice
Tim Griesenbeck, Texas A&M

TACKLES
Louis Jordan, Texas
Ox Ford, Texas A&M
Bibb Falk, Texas

GUARDS
Dutch Hohn, Texas A&M
E.S. Wilson, Texas A&M

CENTER
Pig Dittmar, Texas

BACKS
Joe Utay, Texas A&M
Clyde Littlefield, Texas
Jack Mahan, Texas A&M
Blue Rattan, TCU
Benny Winkleman, Arkansas
Cecil Grigg, Austin College

1920-1929

ENDS
Rags Matthews, TCU
Wear Schoonover, Arkansas
Puny Wilson, Texas A&M

TACKLES
Marion (Scrapiron) Hammon, SMU
Russ Blailock, Baylor
Gordy Brown, Texas

GUARDS
Mike Brumbelow, TCU
Choc Sanders, SMU
Wash Underwood, Rice

CENTER
Johnny Washmon, TCU
Noble Atkins, TCU

BACKS
Joel Hunt, Texas A&M
Cy Leland, TCU
Howard Grubbs, TCU
Gerald Mann, SMU
Wesley Bradshaw, Baylor
Dexter Shelley, Texas
Smack Reisor, SMU

1930-1939

ENDS
Walter Roach, TCU
Sam Boyd, Baylor
Jim Benton, Arkansas

TACKLES
Truman Spain, SMU
I.B. Hale, TCU
Joe Boyd, Texas A&M

GUARDS
Barton (Bochey) Koch, Baylor
Joe Routt, Texas A&M
Johnny Vaught, TCU
J.C. (Ironman) Wetsel, SMU

CENTER
Darrell Lester, TCU
Ki Aldrich, TCU

BACKS
Davey O'Brien, TCU
Sam Baugh, TCU
Bobby Wilson, SMU
Harry Shuford, SMU
John Kimbrough, Texas A&M
Harrison Stafford, Texas
Bohn Hilliard, Texas
Bill Wallace, Rice

1940-1949

ENDS
Froggie Williams, Rice
Hub Bechtol, Texas
Mal Kutner, Texas

TACKLES
Derrell Palmer, TCU
Dick Harris, Texas
Clyde Flowers, TCU

GUARDS
Weldon Humble, Rice
Marshall Robnett, Texas A&M
Chal Daniel, Texas

CENTER
Joe Watson, Rice

BACKS
Doak Walker, SMU
Bobby Layne, Texas
Jack Crain, Texas
Pete Layden, Texas
Derace Moser, Texas A&M
Clyde Scott, Arkansas
Lindy Berry, TCU

1950-1959

ENDS
Bill Howton, Rice
Buddy Dial, Rice
Raymond Berry, SMU

TACKLES
Don Floyd, TCU
Charley Krueger, Texas A&M
James Ray Smith, Baylor

GUARDS
Bill Glass, Baylor
Bud McFadin, Texas
Bud Brooks, Arkansas
Harley Sewell, Texas

CENTER
Dick Hightower, SMU
Hugh Pitts, TCU

BACKS
Jim Swink, TCU
John David Crow, Texas A&M
Kyle Rote, SMU
Larry Isbell, Baylor
Dicky Moegle, Rice
Bob Smith, Texas A&M

1960-1969

ENDS
Lawrence Elkins, Baylor

Jerry Levias, SMU
Cotton Speyrer, Texas

TACKLES
Bob Lilly, TCU
Scott Appleton, Texas
Loyd Phillips, Arkansas

GUARDS
Tommy Nobis, Texas
John LaGrone, SMU
Johnny Treadwell, Texas

CENTER
E.J. Holub, Texas Tech

BACKS
James Street, Texas
Duke Carlisle, Texas
Donny Anderson, Texas Tech
Ronnie Bull, Baylor
Lance Alworth, Arkansas
James Saxton, Texas
Chris Gilbert, Texas

1970-1979

OFFENSE

ENDS
Emanuel Tolbert, SMU
Johnny (Lam) Jones, Texas
Chuck Dicus, Arkansas
Mike Renfro, TCU

LINEMEN
Jerry Sisemore, Texas
Bob Simmons, Texas
Dan Irons, Texas Tech
Greg Kolenda, Arkansas

CENTER
Bill Wyman, Texas

BACKS
Earl Campbell, Texas
Roosevelt Leaks, Texas
Steve Worster, Texas
Tommy Kramer, Rice
Curtis Dickey, Texas A&M
Bubba Bean, Texas A&M

DEFENSE

LINEMEN
Brad Shearer, Texas
Wilson Whitley, Houston
Louie Kelcher, SMU
Roger Goree, Baylor
Bill Atessis, Texas
Robert Jackson, Texas A&M

LINEBACKERS
Ed Sinonini, Texas A&M
Garth Ten Napel, Texas A&M
Randy Braband, Texas

BACKS
Pat Thomas, Texas A&M
Robert Popelka, SMU
Johnnie Johnson, Texas
Raymond Clayburn, Texas

KICKERS
Russell Erxleben, Texas
Tony Franklin, Texas A&M
Steve Little, Arkansas

1980-1989

OFFENSE

ENDS
Gerald McNeil, Baylor
Jason Phillips, Houston
James Maness, TCU
Stanley Washington, TCU

LINEMEN
Terry Tausch, Texas
Jim Mabry, Arkansas
Louis Cheek, Texas A&M
Frank Ditta, Baylor
Doug Dawson, Texas

CENTER
Chris Jackson, SMU
Mike Reuther, Texas

BACKS
Kenneth Davis, TCU
Eric Dickerson, SMU
Craig James, SMU
Andre Ware, Houston
James Gray, Texas Tech
Reggie Dupard, SMU
Kevin Murray, Texas A&M

DEFENSE

LINEMEN
Kenneth Sims, Texas
Billy Ray Smith, Arkansas
Tony DeGrate, Texas
Tony Cherico, Arkansas
Harvey Armstrong, SMU

LINEBACKERS
Mike Singletary, Baylor
Johnny Holland, Texas A&M
Jeff Leiding, Texas

BACKS
Jerry Gray, Texas

Mossy Cade, Texas
Russell Carter, SMU
Thomas Everett, Baylor
Steve Atwater, Arkansas

1990-1995

OFFENSE

ENDS
Kelly Blackwell, TCU
Manny Hazard, Houston
Lloyd Hill, Texas Tech
Mike Adams, Texas

LINEMEN
Blake Brockermeyer, Texas
Dan Neil, Texas
Chris Dausin, Texas A&M
Greg Schorp, Texas A&M
Barret Robbins, TCU
Fred Miller, Baylor

BACKS
Darren Lewis, Texas A&M
Greg Hill, Texas A&M
Trevor Cobb, Rice
Bam Morris, Texas Tech
Andre Davis, TCU
Leeland McElroy, Texas A&M
Ricky Williams, Texas
Bucky Richardson Texas A&M
Max Knake, TCU

DEFENSE

LINEMEN
Santana Dotson, Baylor
Tony Brackens, Texas
Sam Adams, Texas A&M
Shane Dronett, Texas
Brandon Mitchell, Texas A&M

LINEBACKERS
Zach Thomas, Texas Tech
Marcus Buckley, Texas A&M
Antonio Armstrong, Texas A&M

BACKS
Aaron Glenn, Texas A&M
Stanley Richard, Texas
Ray Mickens, Texas A&M
Kevin Smith, Texas A&M

KICKERS
Michael Reeder, TCU
Mark Bounds, Texas Tech

Other Highly Rated Teams ...

YEAR	TEAM, RECORD	COACH, TOP PLAYER	SEASON'S RANK, RATING SYSTEM
1926	SMU, 8-0-1	Ray Morrison, Gerald Mann, qb	No. 8, Football Annual
1927	A&M, 8-0-1	Dana X. Bible, Joel Hunt, hb	No. 7, Football Annual
1929	TCU, 9-0-1	Francis Schmidt, Cy Leland, hb	No. 7, AP
1931	SMU, 9-1-1	Ray Morrison, Speedy Mason, hb	No. 7, Football Annual
1932	TCU, 10-0-1	Francis Schmidt, Johnny Vaught, g	No. 4, Football Annual
1934	RICE, 9-1-1	Jimmy Kitts, Bill Wallace, hb	No. 5, Dickinson
1936	TCU, 9-2-2	Dutch Meyer, Sam Baugh, qb	No. 5, Williamson
1940	A&M, 9-1	Homer Norton, John Kimbrough, fb	No. 5, Dickinson
1941	A&M, 9-2	Homer Norton, Derace Moser, hb	No. 6, Williamson
1946	RICE, 9-2	Jess Neely, Weldon Humble, g	No. 6, Williamson
1947	SMU, 9-0-2	Matty Bell, Doak Walker, hb	No. 2, Football Annual
	TEXAS, 10-1	Blair Cherry, Bobby Layne, qb	No. 3. Litkenhous
1948	SMU, 9-1-1	Matty Bell, Doak Walker, hb	No. 5, Williamson
1949	RICE, 10-1	Jess Neely, Froggy Williams, e	No. 5, AP
1950	TEXAS, 9-2	Blair Cherry, Bud McFadin, g	No. 2, UP
1951	BAYLOR, 8-2-1	George Sauer, Larry Isbell, qb	No. 6, Williamson
1953	RICE, 9-2	Jess Neely, Dicky Moegle, hb	No. 6, AP
1955	TCU, 9-2	Abe Martin, Jim Swink, hb	No. 3, Litkenhous
1956	A&M, 9-0-1	Bear Bryant, John David Crow, hb	No. 5, AP

1959	TEXAS, 9-2	Darrell Royal, Rene Ramirez, hb	No. 4, AP
	TCU, 8-3	Abe Martin, Bob Lilly, t	No. 7, AP
1962	TEXAS, 9-1-1	Darrell Royal, Ernie Koy, hb	No. 4, AP
	ARKANSAS, 9-2	Frank Broyles, Billy Moore, qb	No. 6, AP
1964	TEXAS, 10-1	Darrell Royal, Tommy Nobis, g	No. 5, AP
1965	ARKANSAS, 10-1	Frank Broyles, Bobby Burnett, fb	No. 2, UP
1969	ARKANSAS, 9-2	Frank Broyles, Bill Montgomery, qb	No. 3, UPI
1972	TEXAS, 10-1	Darrell Royal, Roosevelt Leaks, fb	No. 3, AP
1975	TEXAS, 10-2	Darrell Royal, Earl Campbell, fb	No. 6, AP
1976	HOUSTON, 10-2	Bill Yeoman, Wilson Whitley, t	No. 4, AP
1979	HOUSTON, 11-1	Bill Yeoman, Terald Clark, hb	No. 5, AP
1983	TEXAS, 11-1	Fred Akers, Jerry Gray, db	No. 5, AP
1984	SMU, 10-2	Bobby Collins, Reggie Dupard, hb	No. 6, Sagarin
1985	A&M, 10-2	Jackie Sherrill, Kevin Murray, qb	No. 6, AP
1992	A&M, 12-1	R.C. Slocum, Greg Hill, hb	No. 6, CNN/USA Today
1993	A&M, 10-2	R.C. Slocum, Rodney Thomas, hb	No. 6, UPI
1994	A&M, 10-0-1	R.C. Slocum, Leeland McElroy, hb	No. 8, AP

THE HONORS GROUP

*Who threw it, who ran it, who caught it,
who kicked it, who tackled it, who blocked it, and
who might have got himself some kind of a bronze
deal for doing it.*

National Statistical Champions from the Southwest Conference

TOTAL OFFENSE
1938---Davey O'Brien, TCU
1976---Tommy Kramer, Rice
1978---Mike Ford, SMU
1989---Andre Ware, Houston
1990---David Klingler, Houston
1992---Jimmy Klingler, Houston

RUSHING
1929---Cy Leland, TCU
1955---Jim Swink, TCU
1977---Earl Campbell, Texas

PASSING
1935---Sam Baugh, TCU
1936---Sam Baugh, TCU
1937---Davey O'Brien, TCU
1938---Davey O'Brien, TCU
1939---Kay Eakin, Arkansas
1947---Bobby Layne, Texas
1949---Adrian Burk, Baylor
1958---Buddy Humphrey, Baylor
1962---Don Trull, Baylor
1963---Don Trull, Baylor
1968---Chuck Hixson, SMU
1976---Tommy Kramer, Rice

SCORING
1927---Joel Hunt, Texas A&M
1955---Jim Swink, TCU
1977---Earl Campbell, Texas
1993---Bam Morris, Texas Tech

ALL-PURPOSE RUNNING
1955---Jim Swink, TCU
1964---Donny Anderson, Texas Tech
1977---Earl Campbell, Texas

PASS RECEIVING
1937---Jim Benton, Arkansas
1938---Sam Boyd, Baylor
1939---Don Looney, TCU
1942---Bill Rogers, Texas A&M
1963---Lawrence Elkins, Baylor
1987---Jason Phillips, Houston
1988---Jason Phillips, Houston
1989---Manny Hazard, Houston
1990---Manny Hazard, Houston
1991---Freddie Gilbert, Houston
1992---Sherman Smith, Houston,
Lloyd Hill, Texas Tech

PUNTING
1935---Sam Baugh, TCU
1936---Sam Baugh, TCU
1943---Harold Cox, Arkansas
1945---Red Maley, SMU
1957---Dave Sherer, SMU
1963---Danny Thomas, SMU
1969---Ed Marsh, Baylor
1976---Russell Erxleben, Texas
1978---Maury Buford, Texas Tech
1980---Steve Cox, Arkansas
1986---Greg Horne, Arkansas
1991---Mark Bounds, Texas Tech

PUNT RETURNS
1937---Davey O'Brien, TCU
1943---Marion Flanagan, Texas A&M
1947---Lindy Berry, TCU
1948---George Sims, Baylor
1952---Horton Nesrsta, Rice
1954---Dicky Moegle, Rice
1960---Lance Alworth, Arkansas
1961---Lance Alworth, Arkansas
1963---Ken Hatfield, Arkansas
1964---Ken Hatfield, Arkansas
1966---Don Bean, Houston
1993---Aaron Glenn, Texas A&M

KICKOFF RETURNS
1947---Doak Walker, SMU
1972---Larry Williams, Texas Tech
1984---Keith Henderson, Texas Tech
1993---Leeland McElroy, Texas A&M

INTERCEPTIONS
1938---Elmer Tarbox, Texas Tech
1962---Byron Beaver, Houston
1976---Anthony Francis, Houston
1980---Vann McElroy, Baylor
1989---Cornelius Price, Houston
1990---Jerry Parks, Houston

FIELD GOALS
1976---Tony Franklin, Texas A&M
1979---Ish Ordonez, Arkansas
1981---Bruce Lahay, Arkansas
1988---Kendall Trainor, Arkansas
1989---Roman Anderson, Houston
1995---Michael Reeder, TCU

National Award Winners of the Southwest Conference

HEISMAN TROPHY
1938---Davey O'Brien, TCU
1948---Doak Walker, SMU
1957---John David Crow, Texas A&M
1977---Earl Campbell, Texas
1989---Andre Ware, Houston
1998---Ricky Williams, Texas ('95)

MAXWELL AWARD
(Player of Year)

1938---Davey O'Brien, TCU
1947---Doak Walker, SMU
1965---Tommy Nobis, Texas
1998---Ricky Williams, Texas ('95)

WALTER CAMP AWARD
(Player of Year)

1938---Davey O'Brien, TCU
1957---John David Crow, Texas A&M
1977---Earl Campbell, Texas

OUTLAND TROPHY
(Lineman of Year)

1954---Bud Brooks, Arkansas
1963---Scott Appleton, Texas
1965---Tommy Nobis, Texas
1966---Loyd Phillips, Arkansas
1977---Brad Shearer, Texas

LOMBARDI TROPHY
(Lineman of Year)

1976---Wilson Whitley, Houston
1981---Kenneth Sims, Texas
1984---Tony DeGrate, Texas

Kyle Rote of SMU on his 1949 rampage against Notre Dame.

DAVEY O'BRIEN NATIONAL QUARTERBACK AWARD

1989---Andre Ware, Houston

DOAK WALKER NATIONAL RUNNING BACK AWARD

1991---Trevor Cobb, Rice
1993---Bam Morris, Texas Tech
1996---Byron Hanspard, Texas Tech ('94, '95)
1997---Ricky Williams, Texas ('95)
1998---Ricky Williams, Texas ('95)

JIM THORPE AWARD
(Defensive Back of Year)

1986---Thomas Everett, Baylor

LOU GROZA AWARD
(Placekicker of Year)

1995---Michael Reeder, TCU

Southwest Conference Players in the National College Football Hall of Fame
(Position and Best Season listed)

TCU

Davey O'Brien, quarterback, 1938
Sam Baugh, quarterback, 1936
Jim Swink, halfback, 1955
Bob Lilly, tackle, 1960
Ki Aldrich, center, 1938
Darrell Lester, center, 1935
Johnny Vaught, guard, 1932
Rags Matthews, end, 1927

TEXAS

Bobby Layne, quarterback, 1947
Earl Campbell, fullback, 1977
Tommy Nobis, guard, 1965
James Saxton, halfback, 1961
Harrison Stafford, halfback, 1932
Mal Kutner, end, 1941
Bud McFadin, guard, 1950
Hub Bechtol, end, 1946
Bud Sprague, tackle, 1924

TEXAS A&M

John Kimbrough, fullback, 1939
Joe Routt, guard, 1937
John David Crow, halfback, 1957
Joel Hunt, tailback, 1926
Jack Pardee, fullback, 1956
Charlie Krueger, tackle, 1957
Dave Elmendorf, defensive back, 1970
Joe Utay, halfback, 1907

SMU

Doak Walker, tailback, 1948
Bobby Wilson, halfback, 1935
Kyle Rote, halfback, 1950
Don Meredith, quarterback, 1958
Gerald Mann, quarterback, 1926

RICE

Dicky Moegle, halfback, 1954
Weldon Humble, guard, 1946
Froggie Williams, end, 1949
Buddy Dial, end, 1958
Bill Wallace, halfback, 1934

BAYLOR

Mike Singletary, linebacker, 1980
Bochey Koch, guard, 1930
Lawrence Elkins, end, 1964
Bill Glass, guard, 1956
James Ray Smith, tackle, 1954

ARKANSAS

Clyde Scott, halfback, 1948
Lance Alworth, halfback, 1960
Loyd Phillips, tackle, 1966
Wear Schoonover, end, 1929

TEXAS TECH

Donny Anderson, halfback, 1965
E.J. Holub, center, 1960

Southwest Conference Coaches in the National Colege Football Hall of Fame

Dutch Meyer, TCU (1934-1952)
Darrell Royal, Texas (1957-1976)
Dana X. Bible, Texas A&M (1919-1928),
    Texas (1937-1946)
Jess Neely, Rice (1940-1966)
Ray Morrison, SMU (1922-1934)
Homer Norton, Texas A&M (1934-1947)
Morley Jennings, Baylor (1926-1940)
Bear Bryant, Texas A&M (1954-1957)
Frank Broyles, Arkansas (1958-1976)
John W. Heisman, Rice (1924-1927)
Francis Schmidt, Arkansas (1922-1928), TCU
    (1929-1933)
Matty Bell, TCU (1923-1928), Texas A&M
    (1929-1934), SMU (1935-1949)

THE 101 GREATEST SHOOTOUTS IN THE
80-YEAR HISTORY OF THE
SOUTHWEST CONFERENCE
(1915-1995)

1920, Nov. 20, Austin   **TEXAS (8-0) vs. TEXAS A&M (6-0-1)**

The largest football crowd in the state at the time — over 20,000 — jams Clark Field to see the Longhorns hand the Aggies their first loss in two years. Tom Dennis' grab of a tackle-eligible pass leads to Texas' victory.

TEXAS 7, TEXAS A&M 3

1922, Jan. 2, Dallas   **TEXAS A&M (5-1-2) vs. CENTRE (10-0)**

In a State Fair attraction called the Dixie Classic the Aggies' 12th Man tradition is born, and down on the field Puny Wilson and Cap Murrah lead the defense that stops Bo McMillin and the famous Praying Colonels.

TEXAS A&M 22, CENTRE COLLEGE 14

1926, Nov. 25, Dallas   **SMU (7-0-1) vs TCU (6-0-2)**

The Frogs miss a last-second field goal and the conference champion Mustangs survive behind Gerald Mann, "the Little Red Arrow."

SMU 14, TCU 13

1927, Oct. 22, Fort Worth   **TEXAS A&M (4-0) vs. TCU (3-0-1)**

In a battle of unbeatens, called "the biggest event in Fort Worth history" at the time, Rags Matthews leads the goal-line stands that stop Joel Hunt, and Frogs tie one of A&M's greatest teams.

TCU 0, TEXAS A&M 0

1929, Nov. 16, Austin   **TCU (6-0) vs. TEXAS (5-0-2)**

Cy Leland's 95-yard kick return leads the Frogs to their first victory over Texas — and their first conference title — in a thrill-packed game.

TCU 15, TEXAS 12

1932, Nov. 11, Fort Worth   **TCU (7-0-1) vs. TEXAS (6-1)**

The Frogs' all-star line, led by Johnny Vaught, stops Texas' all-star backfield of Harrison Stafford, Ernie Koy, and Bohn Hilliard in this showdown for the championship.

TCU 14, TEXAS 0

1934, Oct. 6, Lafayette, Ind.   **RICE (1-0-1) vs. PURDUE (0-0)**

The Owls' Bill Wallace and John McCauley outshine All-America Duane Purvis and stun Purdue, the nation's preseason favorite for No. 1.

RICE 14, PURDUE 0

1934, Oct. 6, South Bend   **TEXAS (2-0) vs. NOTRE DAME (0-0)**

On the same day in the same state, Bohn Hilliard leads Texas to a shocking upset over Notre Dame. Combined with Rice's win over Purdue, it draws much national attention to the Southwest Conference.

TEXAS 7, NOTRE DAME 6

1934, Oct. 27, Houston   **RICE (4-0-1) vs. TEXAS (4-1)**

The fierce demand for tickets creates the conference's first game-of-the-week radio broadcast. Wallace and McCauley outduel Bohn Hilliard.

RICE 20, TEXAS 9

1935, Oct. 19, Dallas   **RICE (4-0) vs. SMU (4-0)**

More than 30,000 pack 25,000-seat Ownby Stadium as the No. 1 Owls come to town talking about their own Wallace and McCauley — and leave talking about SMU's Bobby Wilson and Harry Shuford.

SMU 10, RICE 0

1935, Nov. 30, Fort Worth   TCU (10-0) vs. SMU (10-0)
Bobby Wilson edges Sam Baugh in the Game of the Year, Decade, and Century. TCU's 30,000-seat stadium spills over with 42,000. National title and Rose Bowl bid at stake, coast-to-coast radio.
SMU 20, TCU 14

1936, Jan. 1, Rose Bowl   SMU (12-0) vs. STANFORD (7-1)
The only Rose Bowl appearance by a SWC team. But the heavily favored Mustangs fumble the game away to Bobby Grayson and cohorts.
STANFORD 7, SMU 0

1936, Jan. 1, Sugar Bowl   TCU (11-1) vs. LSU (9-1)
The Frogs grab a national title of their own as Sam Baugh leads TCU to a baseball-score win over the Southeastern Conference champions.
TCU 3, LSU 2

1936, Dec.12, San Francisco   TCU (7-2-2) vs. SANTA CLARA (7-0)
Baugh puts on an aerial show in Kezar Stadium as the Frogs knock off No. 1-ranked Santa Clara, the nation's last undefeated team of '36.
TCU 9, SANTA CLARA 0

1937, Jan. 1, Cotton Bowl   TCU (8-2-2) vs. MARQUETTE (7-1)
The inaugural Cotton Bowl matches two All-America passers, Sam Baugh and Raymond (Buzz) Buivid, in yet another quarterback duel. Slingin' makes it no contest.
TCU 16, MARQUETTE 6

1938, Jan. 1, Cotton Bowl   RICE (5-3-2) vs. COLORADO (8-0)
Sophomores Ernie Lain and Ollie Cordill, Rice's newest Touchdown Twins, prove too much for Colorado's All-America Whizzer White.
RICE 28, COLORADO 14

1938, Oct. 29, Fort Worth   TCU (5-0) vs. BAYLOR (4-0-1)
The season's long-awaited, sold-out Game of the Year matches Davey O'Brien against Baylor's "Bullet Bill" Patterson. It's close at the half, but O'Brien's passes make it a runaway, and the Frogs head for No. 1.
TCU 39, BAYLOR 7

1939, Jan. 2, Sugar Bowl   TCU (10-0) vs. CARNEGIE TECH (7-1)
O'Brien's passing, running, and field goal carry No. 1 TCU past No. 5 Carnegie Tech, the powerhouse of the East, in a great game.
TCU 15, CARNEGIE TECH 7

1939, Oct. 14, Tyler, Texas   TEXAS A&M (3-0) vs. VILLANOVA (2-0)
In an attraction of the "Tyler Rose Festival," John Kimbrough and the Aggies indicate they be something special as they overwhelm a famed Eastern team that hasn't lost a game in three seasons.
TEXAS A&M 33, VILLANOVA 7

1940, Jan. 1, Sugar Bowl   TEXAS A&M (10-0) vs. TULANE (8-0-1)
End Herbie Smith blocks an extra point and the Kimbrough-led national champion Aggies come from behind to nip the Green Wave.
TEXAS A&M 14, TULANE 13

1940, Nov. 9, Dallas   TEXAS A&M (6-0) vs. SMU (4-0-1)
In the Game of the Year, Kimbrough plows through the mud to give the Aggies a fourth-quarter win over a tough SMU team led by tailback Ray Mallouf and fullback Presto Johnston.
TEXAS A&M 19, SMU 7

1940, Nov. 28, Austin   TEXAS A&M (8-0) vs. TEXAS (6-2)
Pete Layden, Jack Crain, and Noble Doss guide the Longhorns to a legendary upset over an Aggie team that had won 19 straight and was clearly headed for the Rose Bowl.
TEXAS 7, TEXAS A&M 0

1941, Jan. 1, Cotton Bowl   TEXAS A&M (8-1) vs. FORDHAM (7-1)

Marion Pugh's long touchdown pass to 'Bama Smith on a "hideout play" combines with Kimbrough to top the rugged Rams.
TEXAS A&M 13, FORDHAM 12

1941, Nov. 15, Austin   TEXAS (6-0-1) vs. TCU (5-2)

Dean Bagley's 55-yard run and Emery Nix's last-minute pass to Van Hall shocks Texas' talented No. 1-ranked team that's just been splashed on the cover of *Life* magazine.
TCU 14, TEXAS 7

1941, Nov. 27, College Station TEXAS A&M (9-0) vs. TEXAS (6-1-1)

The Longhorns regain their stride and bury the undefeated Aggies behind Jack Crain, Pete Layden, and Spec Sanders. A week later, they pound Oregon 71-7 and finish with the No. 1 ranking from Williamson.
TEXAS 23, TEXAS A&M 0

1942, Jan. 1, Orange Bowl   GEORGIA (8-1-1) vs. TCU (7-2-1)

Frank Sinkwich has his greatest day as the Bulldogs outlast a TCU rally sparked by triple-threat Kyle Gillespie. It's the first appearance for a Southwest Conference team in the Orange Bowl.
GEORGIA 40, TCU 26

1943, Jan. 1, Cotton Bowl   TEXAS (8-2) vs. GEORGIA TECH (9-1)

First post-season game for the Longhorns and they make the most of it as Roy Dale McKay and Jackie Field get the best of No. 5 Georgia Tech's young All-America star, Clint Castleberry.
TEXAS 14, GEORGIA TECH 7

1946, Jan. 1, Cotton Bowl   TEXAS (9-1) vs. MISSOURI (6-3)

Sophomore Bobby Layne accounts for all of Texas' points when he rushes for three touchdowns, passes for two, catches a touchdown pass, and boots four extra points. It's still a bowl-game record.
TEXAS 40, MISSOURI 27

1946, Oct. 26, Houston   TEXAS (5-0) vs. RICE (3-1)

Bobby Layne and the Steers are No. 1 and averaging 42 points a game but it all ends with a thud when the Owls' Virgil Eikenberg flips a late touchdown pass to end Windell Williams.
RICE 18, TEXAS 13

1947, Jan. 1, Orange Bowl   RICE (8-2) vs. TENNESSEE (9-1)

Guard Weldon Humble confirms his All-America status as he leads a Rice defense that obliterates the Vols' single wing attack.
RICE 8, TENNESSEE 0

1947, Nov. 1, Dallas   TEXAS (6-0) vs. SMU (5-0)

Doak Walker vs. Bobby Layne. Most frantic ticket demand since the TCU-SMU game of '35 moves the contest to the Cotton Bowl. A Game of the Decade that lives up to expectations, and Doak's heroics win it.
SMU 14, TEXAS 13

1947, Nov. 29, Fort Worth   SMU (9-0) vs. TCU (4-4-1)

It takes Doak Walker's greatest game to enable the Ponies to tie Lindy Berry and the upset-minded Frogs in the final seconds.
SMU 19, TCU 19

1948, Jan. 1, Sugar Bowl   TEXAS (9-1) vs. ALABAMA (8-2)

It's billed as a battle between two brilliant quarterbacks, Bobby Layne and Harry Gilmer, but Texas has far more than Layne.
TEXAS 27, ALABAMA 7

1949, Jan. 1, Cotton Bowl   SMU (8-1-1) vs. OREGON (9-1)

Doak Walker and Kyle Rote's all-around play outclasses the passes of Norm Van Brocklin.
SMU 21, OREGON 13

1949, Nov. 26, Houston   **RICE (8-1) vs. BAYLOR (8-1)**

The best team in Rice history — Tobin Rote, Froggie Williams, Joe Watson, et al. — prove too much for Adrian Burk, the nation's leading passer, and one of Baylor's finest teams. The title goes to Rice.

     RICE 21, BAYLOR 7

1949, Dec. 3, Dallas   **SMU (5-3-1) vs. NOTRE DAME (9-0)**

The No. 1 Irish come to Dallas for a long-awaited intersectional affair. Doak Walker is injured and on the sideline, but Kyle Rote's amazing performance almost trips up the national champions.

     NOTRE DAME 27, SMU 20

1950, Sept. 30, Columbus, O.   **SMU (1-0) vs. OHIO STATE (0-0)**

Fred Benners' passes and Kyle Rote's running outlast Vic Janowicz and the favored Buckeyes in a wild one.

     SMU 32, OHIO STATE 28

1950, Nov. 4, Austin   **SMU (5-0) vs. TEXAS (4-1)**

SMU arrives as the nation's No. 1 team and with Kyle Rote currently on the cover of *Life*, but the Ponies are overwhelmed by Byron Townsend's rushing, Bud McFadin's defense, and Texas' overall power.

     TEXAS 23, SMU 20

1951, Oct. 20, Fort Worth   **TEXAS A&M (4-0) vs. TCU (2-2)**

Ray McKown miraculously produces three touchdowns in the last seven minutes to shock All-America Bob Smith and the highly rated Aggies.

     TCU 20, TEXAS A&M 14

1952, Nov. 8, Waco   **BAYLOR (4-1-1) vs. TEXAS (5-2)**

Two glittering backfields go on a bizarre scoring spree. When it's over, Texas' Gib Dawson, Dick Ochoa, T Jones, and Billy Quinn have edged out Baylor's Jerry Coody and L.G. Dupre on a touchdown in the last 40 seconds.

     TEXAS 35, BAYLOR 33

1954, Jan. 1, Cotton Bowl   **RICE (8-2) vs. ALABAMA (6-2-3)**

Despite Tommy Lewis' off-the-bench tackle, Rice's Dicky Moegle is too much for No. 8 Alabama.

     RICE 28, ALABAMA 6

1954, Oct. 23, Little Rock   **ARKANSAS (4-0) vs. MISSISSIPPI (5-0)**

One of Arkansas' great intersectional wins. Preston Carpenter catches a 66-yard "Powder River" pass from Buddy Bob Benson and suddenly the Ole Miss Rebels are no longer contending for No. 1.

     ARKANSAS 6, MISSISSIPPI 0

1955, Nov. 12, Austin   **TCU (7-1) vs. TEXAS (4-4)**

In the decisive conference game, TCU's All-America Jim Swink has one of those Red Grange days — 235 yards gained and broken-field touchdown scampers of 67, 55, and 47 yards.

     TCU 47, TEXAS 20

1956, Oct. 20, College Station   **TCU (3-0) vs. TEXAS A&M (3-0-1)**

The "Hurricane Game." It's John David Crow vs. Jim Swink. National title hopes for both teams. Two TCU scores are denied by penalties, a violent storm interrupts, and Crow scores on a late drive to break Purple hearts.

     TEXAS A&M 7, TCU 6

1957, Jan. 1, Cotton Bowl   **TCU (7-3) vs. SYRACUSE (7-1)**

Chuck Curtis' passes and Jim Swink's dashes are more than the equal of Jim Brown's running. It's not that close.

     TCU 28, SYRACUSE 27

1957, Jan. 1, Sugar Bowl   **TENNESSEE (10-0) vs. BAYLOR (8-2)**

Behind Dal Shofner's halfback play and Bill Glass' defense, the Bears upset All-America Johnny Majors and the nation's No. 2 team.

     BAYLOR 13, TENNESSEE 7

1957, Sept. 28, Columbus, O.   TCU (0-0-1) vs. OHIO STATE (0-0)

The lead changes hands five times and Jim Shofner's 90-yard punt return proves the difference as the Frogs upset the eventual national champions.

TCU 18, OHIO STATE 14

1957, Nov. 16, Houston   TEXAS A&M (8-0) vs. RICE (4-3)

King Hill and Buddy Dial lead the Owls to a shocking upset over John David Crow and the nation's No. 1 team.

RICE 7, TEXAS A&M 6

1958, Oct. 10, Dallas   TEXAS (3-0) vs. OKLAHOMA (2-0)

In the first year of the 2-point conversion rule, the Longhorns of Bobby Lackey and Rene Ramirez pull one off to hand the No. 2-ranked Sooners their only loss of the year.

TEXAS 15, OKLAHOMA 14

1959, Nov. 14, Austin   TEXAS (8-0) vs. TCU (5-2)

The defensive play of Bob Lilly and Don Floyd and Harry Moreland's 56-yard fourth-quarter scoring run knock off the No. 2 Longhorns and give TCU a share of the conference title.

TCU 14, TEXAS 9

1960, Jan. 1, Cotton Bowl   TEXAS (9-1) vs. SYRACUSE (10-0)

The Longhorns make it interesting for a while but Ernie Davis and powerful No. 1 Syracuse have too many weapons.

SYRACUSE 23, TEXAS 14

1961, Nov. 18, Austin   TEXAS (8-0) vs. TCU (2-3-2)

A 50-yard pass from Sonny Gibbs to Buddy Iles jolts Texas out of the No. 1 ranking. One of the biggest upsets in SWC history.

TCU 6, TEXAS 0

TCU's Dean Bagley, far left, winds up his 55-yard td against Texas in 1941.

1962, Jan. 1, Cotton Bowl   TEXAS (9-1) vs. MISSISSIPPI (9-1)

While James Saxton, Mike Cotten, and Jack Collins do the damage on offense, Texas' defense, led by Jerry Cook, intercepts five Ole Miss passes. Longhorns win the best Cotton Bowl to date.

TEXAS 12, MISSISSIPPI 7

1962, Oct. 20, Austin   TEXAS (4-0) vs. ARKANSAS (4-0)

Longhorn-Razorback shootouts are now in fashion. In this one, Texas' Johnny Treadwell, Pat Culpepper, and pals specialize in goal-line stands and win a fierce battle of unbeatens.

TEXAS 7, ARKANSAS 3

1963, Oct. 12, Dallas   TEXAS (3-0) vs. OKLAHOMA (2-0)

Oklahoma, led by Joe Don Looney, comes into the game ranked No. 1 and discovers that the Longhorns of Duke Carlisle, Tommy Ford, and Tommy Nobis are the real No. 1.

TEXAS 28, OKLAHOMA 7

1963, Nov. 9, Austin   TEXAS (7-0) vs. BAYLOR (5-1)

With the No. 1 ranking at stake, Carlisle, Ford, Nobis and the others overcome Baylor's aerial combo of Don Trull-Lawrence Elkins. Carlisle's last-minute interception saves the day for Texas.

TEXAS 7, BAYLOR 0

1964, Jan. 1, Cotton Bowl   TEXAS (10-0) vs. NAVY (9-1)

It's No. 1 vs. No. 2 and Duke Carlisle outpasses Heisman winner Roger Staubach as the Middies are out-manned and outcoached.

TEXAS 28, NAVY 6

1964, Oct. 17, Austin   TEXAS (4-0) vs. ARKANSAS (4-0)

Ken Hatfield's punt return for a touchdown and Texas' failure to make a 2-point conversion sends the national championship to the Ozarks.

ARKANSAS 14, TEXAS 13

1965, Jan. 1, Orange Bowl   TEXAS (9-1) vs. ALABAMA (10-0)

Ernie Koy leads the attack and Tommy Nobis spearheads a defense that stops Joe Namath and No. 1 Alabama at the goal in a classic.

TEXAS 21, ALABAMA 17

1965, Jan. 1, Cotton Bowl   ARKANSAS (10-0) vs. NEBRASKA (9-1)

Fred Marshall engineers a fourth-quarter drive and Bobby Burnett plows over for the winning touchdown in the last four minutes as the Hogs earn the Football Writers' award for the national championship.

ARKANSAS 10, NEBRASKA 7

1965, Oct. 16, Fayetteville   TEXAS (4-0) vs. ARKANSAS (4-0)

In one of the most exciting shootouts of all, No. 1 Texas comes from 20 points down to take the lead, only to have Jon Brittenum and Bobby Crockett stage their own comeback in the final seconds.

ARKANSAS 27, TEXAS 24

1968, Jan. 1, Cotton Bowl   ALABAMA (8-1-1) vs. TEXAS A&M (6-4)

Pupil tops teacher. Aggie Coach Gene Stallings had played for Bear Bryant at A&M. Now Stallings' Aggies, led by Edd Hargett, upset Bryant's Ken Stabler-led Crimson Tide.

TEXAS A&M 20, ALABAMA 16

1968, Oct. 19, Austin   TEXAS (2-1-1) vs. ARKANSAS (4-0)

James Street and Chris Gilbert thoroughly establish the Wishbone as they outscore the unbeaten Hogs and start their drive toward three straight national titles.

TEXAS 39, ARKANSAS 29

1968, Dec. 31, Bluebonnet Bowl   SMU (7-3) vs. OKLAHOMA (7-3)

Jerry Levias and Mike Richardson lead the Mustangs over the favored Sooners in a scoring battle.

SMU 28, OKLAHOMA 27

1969, Dec. 6, Fayetteville   TEXAS (9-0) vs. ARKANSAS (9-0)

The mother of all shootouts, national title at stake. James Street's running and passing and a 2-point conversion overcome Bill Montgomery and a 14-point Arkansas lead in the "Game of the Century."
TEXAS 15, ARKANSAS 14

1970, Jan. 1, Cotton Bowl   TEXAS (10-0) vs. NOTRE DAME (8-1-1)

One of the greatest bowl games of all time. Jame Street ignites a late drive that defeats Joe Theismann and the Irish.
TEXAS 21, NOTRE DAME 17

1970, Oct. 3, Austin   TEXAS (2-0) vs. UCLA (3-0)

A 45-yard touchdown pass — Eddie Phillips to Cotton Speyrer — in the game's last 20 seconds saves the day for Texas' unbeaten string. .
TEXAS 20, UCLA 17

1971, Jan. 1, Cotton Bowl   TEXAS (10-0) vs. NOTRE DAME (9-1)

The Irish defense jars the Longhorns into six fumbles, and Joe Theismann's passing completes the upset. Texas' winning streak ends at 30.
NOTRE DAME 24, TEXAS 11

1973, Jan. 1, Cotton Bowl   TEXAS (9-1) vs. ALABAMA (10-1)

Roosevelt Leaks and Alan Lowry lead Texas to another upset of a top-rated Alabama team. This one leaves Darrell Royal with a 3-0-1 lifetime record over Bear Bryant.
TEXAS 17, ALABAMA 13

1973, Dec. 29, Gator Bowl   TEXAS TECH (10-1) vs. TENNESSEE (8-3)

Quarterback Joe Barnes and end Andre Tillman complete one of the Red Raiders' finest seasons with a victory in Jacksonville.
TEXAS TECH 28, TENNESSEE 19

John David Crow, Darrell Royal, Doak Walker, and Dan Jenkins — in the presence of the author's heroes.

1974, Nov. 9, Waco **BAYLOR (5-3) vs. TEXAS (6-2)**

Neal Jeffrey and Steve Beaird bring Baylor back from a 24-7 halftime deficit for the victory that earns the Bears their first conference championship in 50 years.

BAYLOR 34, TEXAS 24

1975, Nov. 28, College Station TEXAS A&M (9-0) vs. TEXAS (9-1)

Bubba Bean has a big day rushing against Earl Campbell and the Aggies find themselves on the brink of a possible national championship.

TEXAS A&M 20, TEXAS 10

1975, Dec. 6, Little Rock **TEXAS A&M (10-0) vs. ARKANSAS (9-2)**

Never does a dream crash with such a noise. Scott Bull and Ike Forte send the injured Aggies reeling and snatch a share of the conference crown.

ARKANSAS 31, TEXAS A&M 6

1976, Oct. 30, Lubbock **TEXAS TECH (5-0) vs. TEXAS (3-1-1)**

Larry Isaac provides the running punch as the Red Raiders outscore Darrell Royal's last Texas team.

TEXAS TECH 31, TEXAS 28

1976, Nov. 30, Lubbock **TEXAS TECH (8-0) vs. HOUSTON (7-2)**

Danny Davis wins the quarterback duel from Texas Tech's Rodney Allison, and the Cougars capture the title in their first season as a Southwest Conference member.

HOUSTON 27, TEXAS TECH 19

1977, Oct. 8, Dallas **TEXAS (3-0) vs. OKLAHOMA (4-0)**

Randy McEachern comes out of obscurity to quarterback Texas to a win over No. 2 Oklahoma. Earl Campbell rushes for 124 yards, starts his drive to the Heisman.

TEXAS 13, OKLAHOMA 6

1977, Oct. 15, Fayetteville **TEXAS (4-0) vs. ARKANSAS (4-0)**

Texas' second Poll Bowl in a row features a rushing duel between Earl Campbell and Ben Cowins. The Steers win another biggie.

TEXAS 13, ARKANSAS 9

1978, Jan. 2, Cotton Bowl **TEXAS (11-0) vs. NOTRE DAME (10-1)**

The Irish behind Joe Montana score easily and often and virtually manhandle the nation's No. 1 team. Texas looks woefully unprepared.

NOTRE DAME 38, TEXAS 10

1978, Jan. 2, Orange Bowl **ARKANSAS (10-1) vs. OKLAHOMA (10-1)**

Meanwhile, after Lou Holtz suspends three of his own players, his Razorbacks unleash Roland Sales and score a shocker over No. 2 Oklahoma.

ARKANSAS 31, OKLAHOMA 6

1979, Jan. 1, Cotton Bowl **HOUSTON (9-2) vs. NOTRE DAME (8-3)**

Danny Davis has Houston up 34-12 with only seven minutes left in a game played in subzero weather, but that's enough time for Joe Montana to mount an incredible comeback and win in the last 2 seconds.

NOTRE DAME 35, HOUSTON 34

1979, Nov. 10, Houston **HOUSTON (8-0) vs. TEXAS (6-1)**

Seven times Houston comes from behind to win games this season, but this isn't one of them. The Longhorns of A.J. (Jam) Jones and Johnny (Lam) Jones put the only blemish on the Cougars' record.

TEXAS 21, HOUSTON 13

1980, Jan. 1, Cotton Bowl **HOUSTON (10-1) vs. NEBRASKA (10-1)**

Another Cotton Bowl comes down to the end for Houston. This time, with 19 seconds left, the Cougars' Terry Elston flips a winning pass from the nine-yard line to uphold the honor of the conference against No. 3 Nebraska.

HOUSTON 17, NEBRASKA 14

1980, Oct. 11, Waco   **BAYLOR (4-0) vs. SMU (4-0)**

Mike Singletary leads the defense, Walter Abercrombie and Jay Jeffrey lead the offense, and Baylor outscores the Mustangs in the crucial game of the conference race.

BAYLOR 32, SMU 28

1981, Oct. 24, Dallas   **SMU (6-0) vs. TEXAS (4-1)**

Kenneth Sims and the Texas defense shut down SMU's all-star backfield — Eric Dickerson, Craig James, Lance McIlhenny — and Robert Brewer quarterbacks the Horns to a victory. Both teams are eventually named national champions by different systems.

TEXAS 9, SMU 7

1982, Jan. 1, Cotton Bowl   **TEXAS (9-1-1) vs. ALABAMA (9-1-1)**

Robert Brewer and Terry Orr bring the Longhorns from 10 points down to an upset over Bear Bryant's No. 3 Crimson Tide.

TEXAS 14, ALABAMA 12

1982, Oct. 23, Austin   **SMU (6-0) vs. TEXAS (3-1)**

Dickerson, James, and McIlhenny enjoy revenge on Texas as the Ponies drive to another national title for new coach Bobby Collins.

SMU 30, TEXAS 17

1983, Jan. 1, Cotton Bowl   **SMU (10-0-1) vs. PITTSBURGH (9-2)**

The Mustangs wind up as the only undefeated team in the land as they outlast Dan Marino and Pitt on a cold New Year's Day.

SMU 7, PITTSBURGH 3

1983, Oct. 22, Dallas   **SMU (5-0) vs. TEXAS (5-0)**

Third chapter in the Longhorn-Mustang saga for national honors finds the no-name Texas offense getting the best of Reggie Dupard, Don King, and a new batch of SMU stars.

TEXAS 15, SMU 12

1984, Jan. 2, Cotton Bowl   **TEXAS (11-0) vs. GEORGIA (9-1-1)**

It would have meant the national championship if Texas could have held onto a 9-3 lead, but a fumbled punt late in the day leads to a crushing Bulldog touchdown.

GEORGIA 10, TEXAS 9

1984, Oct. 6, Fayetteville   **ARKANSAS (2-0-1) vs. TCU (2-1)**

Unbeleeevable. That's what's said of the Frogs all year long as they go from a season of 1-8-2 to a season of 8-3 behind All-America running back Kenneth Davis. It all starts here as TCU comes from 31-17 behind in the last 10 minutes to win with only 15 seconds left on the clock.

TCU 32, ARKANSAS 31

1985, Oct. 19, Waco   **TEXAS A&M (4-1) vs. BAYLOR (5-1)**

First in a two-game series of conference showdowns between two top quarterbacks. Cody Carlson gets an edge over Kevin Murray in this one.

BAYLOR 20, TEXAS A&M 15

1986, Jan. 1, Cotton Bowl   **TEXAS A&M (9-2) vs. AUBURN (8-3)**

The Aggie defense, spearheaded by Johnny Holland, does the job on Bo Jackson and the SEC takes a bruise from the SWC.

TEXAS A&M 36, AUBURN 16

1986, Oct. 18, College Station   **TEXAS A&M (4-1) vs. BAYLOR (4-2)**

Kevin Murray evens the score with Cody Carlson and the Aggies are on the road to another conference title.

TEXAS A&M 31, BAYLOR 30

1988, Jan. 1, Cotton Bowl   **TEXAS A&M (9-2) vs. NOTRE DAME (8-3)**

Kevin Murray pilots the Aggies over Heisman winner Tim Brown, and a Notre Dame team will be the national champion a year later.

TEXAS A&M 35, NOTRE DAME 10

1989, Oct. 28, Little Rock   ARKANSAS (5-1) vs. HOUSTON (5-1)

Barry Foster and the Porkers win a scoreboard festival over the Cougars and Andre Ware, the eventual Heisman winner.
ARKANSAS 45, HOUSTON 39

1990, Nov. 10, Austin   HOUSTON (8-0) vs. TEXAS (6-1)

Quarterback David Klingler and the high-scoring Cougars are aiming at the No. 1 ranking, but Butch Hadnot and Texas outscore the "Run and Shoot" Houston offense — with a little help from their defense.
TEXAS 45, HOUSTON 24

1990, Dec. 29, Holiday Bowl   TEXAS A&M (8-3-1) vs. BYU (10-2)

It doesn't matter that BYU has Ty Detmer, the Heisman winner. The Aggies have All-America runner Darren Lewis, quarterback Bucky Richardson, and more incentive.
TEXAS A&M 65, BRIGHAM YOUNG 14

1993, Jan. 1, Cotton Bowl   TEXAS A&M (12-0) vs. NOTRE DAME (10-1)

Notre Dame blasts the Greg Hill-led Aggies' perfect record with too many guns, namely Rick Mirer and Jerome Bettis.
NOTRE DAME 28, TEXAS A&M 3

1994, Nov. 25, Fort Worth   TCU (6-4) vs. TEXAS TECH (6-4)

Andre Davis' running carries the Frogs on a late touchdown drive to upset the Red Raiders in the season's last game. The victory throws TCU into a five-way tie for the conference championship, the only five-way tie in the history of a major conference.
TCU 24, TEXAS TECH 17

1995, Oct. 21, Austin   TEXAS (4-1-1) vs. VIRGINIA (7-1)

Against this highly ranked team from the Atlantic Coast, James Brown ignites the drive and Texas wins it on Phil Dawson's 50-yard field goal into a 20-mile-per-hour wind on the very last play.
TEXAS 17, VIRGINIA 16

1995, Dec. 2, College Station   TEXAS (9-1-1) vs. TEXAS A&M (8-2)

In the last weekend of the last Southwest Conference season, a Longhorn freshman named Ricky Williams — who'll win the Heisman before he's done — rips off 163 yards, scores twice, and leads Texas to the last championship of the 80-year-old league.
TEXAS 16, TEXAS A&M 6

From the author's office wall.

COLLEGE FOOTBALL'S "TEAM OF THE CENTURY"

(These selections are made by an authority with a keen sense of history and a superior knowledge of the subject matter, plus it's the end of the century and this is the only chance I have to do it, and the only place I have to put it.)

OFFENSE

Quarterback
Sam Baugh, TCU, 1934-36

Halfbacks
Doak Walker, SMU, 1945, 1947-49
Tom Harmon, Michigan, 1938-40

Fullback
O.J. Simpson, Southern Cal, 1967-68

Receivers
Don Hutson, Alabama, 1932-34
Johnny Rodgers, Nebraska, 1970-72

Tackles
George Connor, Notre Dame, 1946-47
Bronko Nagurski, Minnesota, 1927-29

Guards
Bob Suffridge, Tennessee, 1938-40
Jim Parker, Ohio State, 1954-56

Center
Chuck Bednarik, Pennsylvania, 1945-48

Kick Returner
Red Grange, Illinois, 1923-25

DEFENSE

Linemen
Bob Lilly, TCU, 1958-60
Rich Glover, Nebraska, 1970-72
Lee Roy Selmon, Oklahoma, 1972-75
Bubba Smith, Michigan State, 1964-66

Linebackers
Tommy Nobis, Texas, 1963-65
Dick Butkus, Illinois, 1962-64
Lee Roy Jordan, Alabama, 1960-62

Defensive Backs
Ronnie Lott, Southern Cal, 1977-80
Jack Tatum, Ohio State, 1968-70
Jim Thorpe, Carlisle, 1908, 1911-12
Charlie Trippi, Georgia, 1941-42, 1946

Placekicker
John Lee, UCLA, 1982-85

Punter
Russell Erxleben, Texas, 1976-78

Head Coach
Bear Bryant, Alabama

Assistants
Darrell Royal, Texas; Knute Rockne, Notre Dame; Woody Hayes, Ohio State; Frank Leahy, Notre Dame; John McKay, USC; Barry Switzer, Oklahoma.

OFFENSIVE SQUAD

Quarterbacks
Roger Staubach, Navy, 1963-64
Johnny Lujack, Notre Dame, 1943, 1946-47
Bobby Layne, Texas, 1944-47
Charlie Ward, Florida State, 1992-93
Davey O'Brien, TCU, 1936-38
Peyton Manning, Tennessee, 1994-97

Halfbacks
Tony Dorsett, Pittsburgh, 1973-76
Glenn Davis, Army, 1944-46
Billy Cannon, LSU, 1957-59
Billy Sims, Oklahoma, 1976-79
Jim Swink, TCU, 11954-56
Bobby Wilson, SMU, 1933-35
Billy Vessels, Oklahoma, 1950-52
Barry Sanders, Oklahoma, 1986-88

Fullbacks
Jim Brown, Syracuse, 1955-56
Earl Campbell, Texas, 1975-77
Ernie Nevers, Stanford, 1923
John David Crow, Texas A&M, 1955-57
Herschel Walker, Georgia, 1980-82
Ricky Williams, Texas, 1995-98

Receivers
Gaynell Tinsley, LSU, 1934-36
Desmond Howard, Michigan, 1989-91
Brick Muller, California, 1920-22
Keith Jackson, Oklahoma, 1984-87
Froggie Williams, Rice, 1946-49
Bennie Oosterbaan, Michigan, 1925-27
Howard Twilley, Tulsa, 1963-65
Randy Moss, Marshall, 1996-97

Tackles
Fred Sington, Alabama, 1928-30
Bob Gain, Kentucky, 1947-50
Jim Weatherall, Oklahoma, 1949-51
Al Wistert, Michigan, 1947-49
Dick Wildung, Minnesota, 1940-42
DeWitt Coulter, Army, 1944-45
Ron Yary, Southern Cal, 1965-67
Scott Appleton, Texas, 1961-63

Guards
John Hannah, Alabama, 1970-72
Bill Corbus, Stanford, 1931-33

Weldon Humble, Rice, 1941-42, 1946
J.D. Roberts, Oklahoma, 1950-52
Cal Hubbard, Harvard, 1922-23
Calvin Jones, Iowa, 1954-55
Bill Fischer, Notre Dame, 1946-48
Marshall Robnett, Texas A&M, 1939-40

Centers
Dave Rimington, Nebraska, 1979-82
Alex Wojciechowicz, Fordham, 1935-37
Jerry Tubbs, Oklahoma, 1954-56

Kick Returners
Lance Alworth, Arkansas, 1959-61
Nile Kinnick, Iowa, 1938-39
Dicky Moegle, Rice, 1953-54

DEFENSIVE SQUAD

Linemen
Randy White, Maryland, 1972-74
Leon Hart, Notre Dame, 1946-49
Loyd Phillips, Arkansas, 1964-66
Joe Routt, Texas A&M, 1936-37
Harry (Blackjack) Smith, Southern Cal, 1938-39
Mike Reid, Penn State, 1968-69
Hugh Green, Pittsburgh, 1977-80
Bud McFadin, Texas, 1949-50

Linebackers
Brian Bosworth, Oklahoma, 1984-87
Mike Singletary, Baylor, 1977-80
Chris Spielman, Ohio State, 1984-87
Lawrence Taylor, North Carolina, 1977-80
Jerry Robinson, UCLA, 1976-78
George Webster, Michigan State, 1964-66

Defensive Backs
Charles Woodson, Michigan, 1995-97
Bennie Blades, Miami, 1985-87
Deion Sanders, Florida State, 1985-88
Jake Scott, Georgia, 1967-68
Terry Kinard, Clemson, 1979-82
Tommy Casanova, LSU, 1969-71
Ken Easley, UCLA, 1977-80
Jerry Gray, Texas, 1982-84

Placekickers
Kevin Butler, Georgia, 1981-82
Carlos Huerta, Miami, 1988-91
Tony Franklin, Texas A&M, 1976-78

Punters
Ray Guy, Southern Mississippi, 1970-72
Reggie Roby, Iowa, 1981-82
Bill Smith, Ole Miss, 1983-86

"THEY ALL CAME FROM RIGHT AROUND HERE."

Texas hometowns of the early national champions of the Southwest Conference

SMU, 1935

Ends	Maco Stewart	Corsicana
	Bill Tipton	Dallas
Tackles	Truman Spain	Dallas
	Maurice Orr	Hillsboro
Guards	J.C. (Ironman) Wetsel	Dallas
	Billy Stamps	Dallas
Center	Art Johnson	Tyler
Backs	Bobby Wilson	Corsicana
	Harry Shuford	Tyler
	Bob Finley	Corsicana
	Shelley Burt	Hillsboro
	Johnny Sprague	Dallas
	J.R. (Jackrabbit) Smith	Greenville

TCU, 1935

Ends	Walter Roach	Fort Worth
	L.D. Meyer	Waco
Tackles	Drew Ellis	Perryton
	Wilson Groseclose	Abilene
Guards	Tracy Kellow	Lufkin
	Cotton Harrison	Temple
Center	Darrell Lester	Jacksboro
Backs	Sam Baugh	Sweetwater
	Jimmy Lawrence	Harlingen
	Dutch Kline	Gregory
	Tillie Manton	Fort Worth

TCU, 1938

Ends	Don Looney	Sulphur Springs
	Durwood Horner	Fort Worth
Tackles	I.B. Hale	Dallas
	Allie White	Fort Worth
Guards	Forrest Kline	Gregory
	Bud Taylor	Austin
Center	Ki Aldrich	Temple
Backs	Davey O'Brien	Dallas
	Earl Clark	Breckenridge
	Johnny Hall	Kaufman
	Connie Sparks	Panhandle

TEXAS A&M, 1939

Ends	Herbie Smith	San Angelo
	Jim Sterling	Panhandle
Tackles	Joe Boyd	Dallas
	Ernie Pannell	Corsicana
Guards	Marshall Robnett	Klondike
	Chuck Hanke	Kerrville
Center	Tommy Vaughn	Brownwood
Backs	John Kimbrough	Haskell
	Marion Pugh	Fort Worth
	Derace Moser	Stephenville
	Jimmy Thomason	Brownwood
	Cotton Price	Newcastle
	Bill Conatser	Denison

TEXAS, 1941

Ends	Mal Kutner	Dallas	Center	Buddy Jungmichel	Port Arthur
	Preston Flanagan	Longview	Backs	Henry Harkins	Austin
Tackles	Bo Cohenour	Orange		Jack Crain	Nocona
	Julian Garrett	Raymondville		Pete Layden	Dallas
Guards	Chal Daniel	Longview		Noble Doss	Temple
				Vernon Martin	Amarillo

RISE AND FALL OF THE SOUTHWEST CONFERENCE

1915
(Charter members)
Texas
Texas A&M
Baylor
Rice
Arkansas
Oklahoma
Oklahoma A&M
Southwestern U.

1916
(Rice drops out)
Texas
Texas A&M
Baylor
Arkansas
Oklahoma
Oklahoma A&M
Southwestern U.

1917
(Southwestern drops out)
Texas
Texas A&M
Baylor
Arkansas
Oklahoma
Oklahoma A&M

1918-1919
(SMU, Rice admitted)
Texas
Texas A&M
Baylor
Arkansas
Oklahoma
Oklahoma A&M
SMU
Rice

1920
(Oklahoma drops out, Phillips U. joins)
Texas
Texas A&M
Baylor
Arkansas
Oklahoma A&M
SMU
Rice
Phillips U.

1921-1922
(Phillips drops out)
Texas
Texas A&M
Baylor
Arkansas
Oklahoma A&M
SMU
Rice

1923-1924
(TCU admitted)
Texas
Texas A&M
Baylor
Arkansas
Oklahoma A&M
SMU
Rice
TCU

1925-1959
(The 35 years of normalcy)
Texas
Texas A&M
Baylor
Arkansas
SMU
Rice
TCU

1960 -1975
(Texas Tech admitted)
Texas
Texas A&M
Baylor
Arkansas
SMU
Rice
TCU
Texas Tech

1976 -1991
(Houston admitted)
Texas
Texas A&M
Baylor
Arkansas
SMU
Rice
TCU
Texas Tech
Houston

1992 - 1995
(Arkansas Drops out)
Texas
Texas A&M
Baylor
SMU
Rice
TCU
Texas Tech
Houston

THE SAD END

Publisher's dedication . . .

Woodford Press dedicates this book to newspaper sports editors and copy editors, sportswriters and sports photographers everywhere, present and past. I did three hitches in the sports departments of big dailies. In my view there is no tougher job on any newspaper than putting out a Sunday morning sports section on a college football Saturday night. If you learned to enjoy that job you could do any job on any newspaper.

Two things always happened in the sports department on a college football Saturday night. One, you made the critical first-edition deadline even though it looked disastrously impossible an hour earlier. And two, someone would say something that would send the crew into fits of laughter. In my own past, often it was someone like the late, great Stevie Dean, talking to no one in particular as he took occasionally garbled college scores off the wire: "Judas Priest! Bill and Mary beats Ohio State 59-0. Somebody had better investigate that one."

Then at 2 a.m. you walk out into the autumn chill, feeling as if you had just seen a hundred college games all at once, but feeling somehow an important part of it all . . . days of joy and inspiration.

— **David Burgin**
Editor and Publisher